through the woods

through the woods

*making sense
of your spiritual path*

by
J. Clark Saunders

United Church Publishing House

Through the Woods
Making Sense of Your Spiritual Path
J. Clark Saunders

Library and Archives Canada Cataloguing in Publication

Saunders, J. Clark
  Through the woods : making sense of your spiritual path / by J. Clark Saunders.

ISBN 978-1-55134-154-5

  1. Spiritual life—Christianity. 2. Christian life. I. Title.

BV4501.3.S283 2007   248.4   C2006-906542-X

United Church Publishing House
3250 Bloor St. West, Suite 300
Toronto, ON
Canada M8X 2Y4
1-800-268-3781
www.united-church.ca/ucph

Design: Lisa Rebnord, Graphics and Print
Cover photo: DesignPics

Printed in Canada
5   4   3   2   1   11   10   09   08   07   060274

contents

acknowledgements

IN A BOOK THAT SPEAKS OF influences and connections in our experience of life, it is only right that I should acknowledge those whose paths have crossed mine in the preparation of these chapters.

Jim Taylor, Charlotte Caron, Mardi Tindal, and Doug Whiteway were generous in drawing on their experience in writing and publishing as they offered advice and answered questions in the early stages of this project. Lesley Sisler, while believing in the book, was forthright in giving me useful feedback as each chapter was written. A number of people—including members of my own family—were kind enough to allow me to include experiences from their lives, though in some cases their identities remain hidden. The work of Derek Evans and of Marianne Karsh was essential to Chapters 5 and 11 respectively, and I appreciate their willingness to allow me to include some of their reflections. Ashleigh Mitchell kindly provided the vignette that opens Chapter 4, while my daughter Katie is credited with the one that begins Chapter 6.

Much of the writing of the book was undertaken during a sabbatical from my ministry at Westworth United Church in Winnipeg. The sabbatical was a gift. For providing the technological assistance to allow me to write during this period, I am indebted to my cousin John Ledingham. For the gift of space in which to do the writing, I am grateful to my friend Warren McDougall, who opened his home in Toronto to me. And for the gift of time, I thank the people of Westworth in general and my colleague Mona Denton in particular.

The genesis of some of the material in these pages goes back a long way. Courses taught at Naramata Centre in British Columbia as well as discussions in the men's spirituality group, the United Church Women's units, and other study groups at Westworth all turned out—though I may not have known it at the time—to be testing grounds for some of the ideas that have now found their way into print.

Finally, I want to express my thanks to the staff at United Church Publishing House for their encouragement, support, and guidance in bringing this project to a happy conclusion.

encountering the forest

"There is no spot in a forest that does not have its significance; not a clearing, not a thicket that does not have its parallel in the maze of human thought."

SO SAID THE FRENCH WRITER Honoré de Balzac.[1] As I thought of the many meanings, the rich symbolism that our culture and the world of literature have associated with forests, it seemed to me that those meanings could be explored in a book about human experience. In writing it, I have referred to cultural and literary sources, but only as signposts to help readers make sense of the spiritual path of their own lives. Other books about the soul take a therapeutic approach or offer advice about how to develop spiritual practices. My primary objective, however, is to help readers reflect on the elements of already-lived experience in a way that lends meaning and shape to that experience.

The woods we know—or know about—evoke many images and associations, thoughts and feelings. Before reading on, take a few minutes to do a brainstorming exercise: jot down words or phrases that come to mind when you hear the words "forest" or "the woods."

Here are some associations I wrote down myself:

fear	pleasant	don't	trees
dark	cool	wild	shade
mysterious	moist	animals	creek
adventure	smells	untamed	enchanted
dangerous	play	path	magical
unknown	lured	fire	logging

Perhaps you can add to my list from your own. How similar are the two lists? How are they different?

The thought of a forest can bring up an impressive number of associations. In my own list—and perhaps in yours—some are positive and others negative. Some were suggested by ideas about woods and experiences of forests in general; others were inspired by sights, sounds, and smells associated with a particular forest. Perhaps you pictured a dense rainforest on the West Coast, a sparse growth of stunted conifers in thin soil on the rocks of Northern Ontario, or an aspen forest on the Prairies.

The forest is evocative not only in our individual lives, but also in our culture. It is a place to go in search of something, and sometimes what we find is ourselves. We can come to a fork in the path and have to decide which way to go. Unlike towns and cities, which bear the imprint of human life, the forest primeval can seem strange and untamed, suggesting the part of life that is beyond our control. We may be masters here, but we are not masters there. There can be wild animals and monsters in the woods, fears without and fears within to be confronted. In the field of ecology, forests have come to stand for the environment itself; environmentalists are sometimes dismissed as "tree-huggers." The woods can be enchanted, magical places where spells are woven and broken. They can be forbidden places. Don't go in there, we may be told. And yet we do; we must. And when we do, innocence is very often lost.

The woods, in a word, are where life happens. When Henry David Thoreau had spent some time living in the woods at Walden Pond, he produced the book for which he is best remembered: *Walden; or, Life in the Woods*. He wrote, "I went to the woods because I wished to live deliberately, to front only the essential facts of life, and see if I could not learn what it had to teach, and not, when I came to die, discover that I had not lived."[2]

Forests appear in many books—there is the Wild Wood in *The Wind in the Willows* and the Hundred Acre Wood in *Winnie-the-Pooh*. Forests are the subject of songs like the Beatles' "Norwegian Wood" ("Isn't it good?") and children's fare like "The Teddy Bears' Picnic" and "Over the river and through the woods." Movies spanning the gamut from *Bambi* and *Shrek* to *Deliverance* demonstrate how widely the woods can range in human imagination. There are sayings about the forest, too, that apply to certain life situations. Sometimes you "can't see the forest for the trees." Or you're "not out of the woods yet." Many readers will be able to complete the question "If a tree falls in the forest...?" and know exactly what a bear does in the woods.

The Forest in Other Times and Places

Many of the familiar sayings, songs, and stories of forests have their origins in the Western world and in recent centuries, and often in popular culture. But the woods have played a part in human imagination for much longer than that and all over the world. For example, in *Deep in the Familiar*, Joan Cannon Borton describes a tradition from India in which, when his sons had borne sons of their own, a man would leave his family and possessions and live as a hermit in the forest. After raising a family, one entered one's "forest time." This fourth and final stage of life was a time for spiritual practices and reflection, for emancipation from all desire and suffering, for becoming a sage.

The forest figures in arguably the oldest known literary work, the Gilgamesh epic. A hero goes into the forest to slay a demon and, although he succeeds in his mission, arouses the anger of the gods and creates new enemies for himself.

What does the biblical record have to say about forests? The Bible has made foundational contributions to Western culture and literary tradition, and those of us who find food for our souls in it often turn to scripture for spiritual nourishment. But forests are not the first geographical feature that comes to mind in the landscape of the Holy Land. Indeed, the Bible is not noted for its references to forests. And yet, the Hebrew scriptures mention forests more often and with a wider range of associations than one might expect. The forest can be a resource for fuel and building materials, a place of refuge, something to be subdued, the habitat of threatening, destructive animals that seem nonetheless to be part of God's plan, or the scene of fires that speak of wickedness and punishment.

In the New Testament, the woods are conspicuous by their absence. In most English translations, words like "forest" and "woods" do not occur at all. A word that does occur, however, is "wilderness." When, just before Jesus begins his public ministry, the Spirit drives him into the wilderness, he spends 40 days there, tempted by Satan, threatened by wild beasts, and attended by ministering angels. Placing this pivotal event in the landscape of the Middle

East, some translations use the word "desert" in describing it. But as its root suggests, a "wilderness" can be any wild place. In landscapes like that of the Middle East, a wilderness may be assumed to be a desert. But in Europe and North America over the centuries, a wilderness is more likely a forest (another kind of "deserted" place). The Battle of the Wilderness during the American Civil War, for example, was fought in a dense thicket.

That said, the place that a wilderness occupies in the human spirit is essentially the same whether the wilderness is a forest or a desert. It is a place to find solitude, to experience life stripped down to its essentials, to sort out priorities, to be tested or tempted, to get in touch with spiritual things. The desert is such a place for Native Americans of the southwestern states. And the gospel accounts suggest that the desert was such a place for Jesus. But in other parts of the world, the forest can be that sort of wilderness, too.

Moving through ancient to modern times, forests continue to suggest rich meanings and associations. For example, in the classical period in Greece and Rome the forest, in contrast to urban settings, was associated with the supernatural, with disorder and chaos, and with a sense of exile and alienation. Similarly, in ancient Celtic thinking, the woods were the location of the other-world.

Twelfth-century French courtly romances saw the forest's potential for delight, adventure, and escape. The woods could be a good place—provided you had a right to be there. In medieval Europe, a forest would be part of the royal demesne, set aside for hunting and other pleasures that the king would share with his friends. To others it remained forbidden. Trespassers would be prosecuted severely—and poachers, more severely still.

Nevertheless, some outlaws—like Robin Hood—managed to take refuge in forests for long periods. The forest was where Robin Hood hid. Those who in a kind of inverted world were a law unto themselves gave rise to folklore involving wild men and half-human creatures like fairies, trolls, nymphs, and dryads. In medieval culture, those who lived in or near the woods, though clearly human, belonged to a different order from those who lived in a castle or village. Forest people lived both literally and figuratively on the margins of society. Some were outlaws; others were hermits, woodcutters, or swineherds who lived—like many characters later enshrined in fairy-tales—either in a clearing or on the edge of the forest. In medieval England, writes Corinne J. Saunders in *The Forest of Medieval Romance*, the forest was "frequently portrayed in literature as a place of mystery, fear and danger," a place of the unknown or of "menace and encroachment."[3]

Two important Italian writers of the period expanded on these threatening elements. Dante (1265–1321), in the *Divine Comedy*, associated the dark forest with sin, error, and alienation from God. For Dante, writes Robert Pogue Harrison in *Forests: The Shadow of Civilization*, "the forest of moral confusion is deviant, pathless, issueless, terrifying."[4] Earlier medieval writers had feared the animals and brigands who lived in the woods. For Dante, the forest itself became a fearful place. In a later generation, Giovanni Boccaccio (1313–1375) in the *Decameron* narrowed this sinister focus to use the forest as a scene of sexual initiation, carnal knowledge, and the loss of innocence. On the other hand, Boccaccio's contemporary, Petrarch, was inclined to see the forest in more positive terms as a place of refuge and retreat, of peace and introspection.

Over two centuries later, Shakespeare drew upon both the positive and negative roles that forests can play in human imagination. A forest makes a crucial appearance in *Macbeth* when Birnam Wood comes to Dunsinane Hill. Macbeth's enemies cut down branches from the trees for cover as they approach the King's stronghold. As the wood appears to move—as the wild territory of the forest appears to approach a castle, the work of human hands—Macbeth's fate is sealed. But in two comedies—*A Midsummer Night's Dream* and *As You Like It*—the forest plays a more lighthearted role. In these plays, Shakespeare draws on a romantic tradition in which the forest is a place of transformation. Characters who enter the forest find it a place where love, madness, exile, and adventure play a part, but ultimately a transformation takes place. Everyone is changed in some way.

By the time of the 18th-century Enlightenment, forests were no longer exclusively the private playgrounds of kings. They were seen as good things that existed for human benefit, and the need for forest management was beginning to be recognized. However, the motivation for managing a forest was utilitarian. Forests were to be managed not for their own sake, but in order to exploit their resources more effectively for human use.

In the next century, many traditional fairy tales were written down by familiar figures such as the Brothers Grimm. In these tales, writes Harrison, the forest is often the place where the protagonists get lost, meet unusual creatures, undergo spells and transformations, and confront their destinies. Sometimes the forest is a setting for weird enchantments or profound traumas—as, for example, when a child is taken into the woods and abandoned. Typically, though, children "grow up" during their adventures in the forest. Illicit things take place, but lessons are learned. Little Red Ridinghood, for example, resolves at the end of her story never again to stray from the path by herself.

The century and a half that has elapsed since the Brothers Grimm did their work has seen the forest continue to exercise its power on the creative imagination. Through the works of writers and artists and through our own experiences of the woods, the many meanings of the forest continue to speak to the human spirit. And recently, the relationship of human beings to forests and to the ecosystem in general has become a subject of increasing controversy, a controversy that includes a spiritual dimension.

In *Six Walks in the Fictional Woods*, a book about reading and writing fiction, Umberto Eco writes:

> There are two ways of walking through a wood. The first is to try one or several routes (so as to get out of the wood as fast as possible, say, or to reach the house of grandmother, Tom Thumb, or Hansel and Gretel); the second is to walk so as to discover what the wood is like and find out why some paths are accessible and others are not.[5]

As we make our way through the woods, we will try not to rush. Rather, we will take time to observe our surroundings and reflect on our experiences, as we try to make sense of our spiritual paths.

And now, if you are ready, let's begin our journey through the woods.

For personal reflection or group discussion

1. If you can, why not take a walk in a nearby wood? Take your time, noticing the sights, sounds, and smells. What feelings does your sojourn evoke?

   Or, if a literal walk is not possible, take an imaginative walk in a wood that you are familiar with—perhaps one from your childhood. Sit comfortably in a straight-backed chair with your eyes closed, your feet flat on the floor, and your hands resting lightly in your lap. What sights, sounds, and smells come back to you as you imagine yourself in this wood?

   If you do this as a group exercise, talk about it together afterwards.

2. The introduction referred to a number of books, songs, poems, movies, and expressions containing lines about forests. Can you add others? What meanings are attached to the role of forests in these works of imagination?

chapter 1

trailblazers
the ones who have gone ahead

The trail that led through the sparse woods of Whiteshell Provincial Park in eastern Manitoba crossed some of the oldest rocks in the world. Frequently the Precambrian rock burst through the thin layers of soil and vegetation. Sometimes the rocky outcropping spread so far to the left and right, pushing the trees back farther and farther, that I lost the path and had no idea which way to go next. Or I would have had no idea if I hadn't spotted a signpost up ahead. Of the many people who had been this way before me, one—or perhaps a group of two or three—had marked the trail to make the route easier for those who would follow.

THE EXPLORATION OF THE WORLD or the exploration of space, developments in scientific and medical research, the extension of human rights and other social causes—every field has benefited from the pioneers who have blazed its trails. It would be hard to find any area of human endeavour in which someone has started absolutely from scratch, owing nothing to those who have gone before. That is why many books open with an acknowledgements section, to honour the debt owed to those who have laid the groundwork. And perhaps as you read the introduction to this book, some of the symbolic meanings that others have attached to woods and forests had resonance for you.

Trailblazers and Formative Life Stages

If those whose achievements have brought them fame or fortune have had trailblazers to follow, so has each one of us. We have all known people who in one way or another have been a mentor to us: think of people who introduced you to a new career or interest, who recognized a latent talent in you and helped to draw it out, or who influenced your ideas about what is important.

You may be willing to include your parents in your personal list of mentors. Your work, interests, or values—or all of these things—can derive from parental influences. People might even say, "You're walking in your mother's (or father's) footsteps." William Barclay, the Scottish Bible commentator, was happy to acknowledge the influence of his parents. In his memoirs he wrote that there were places in Scotland where he would always—and gladly—be his father's son.

As children pass through adolescence to adulthood, relationships with their parents often become more complex. They are complicated by efforts toward independence and individuality, issues of control and rebellion, and feelings of resentment and frustration. But can you nevertheless acknowledge that you've learned some important things from your parents? It was only after his parents had died that a friend of mine was able to take another look at the hopes they had lodged in him. They really had wanted the best for him, he realized, and had helped equip him for a life that put his gifts to good use.

Yet even the wisest parents cannot give their children everything they need. I come from a long line of male ancestors who were practical men, men who understood how things worked and who were good with their hands: shoemakers, carpenters, and contractors. The talents with which these men were blessed did not come to me, nor did they appear among the gifts that characterized my father. But they were shared in a conspicuous way by my older brother.

When my brother was a teenager and we lived on the West Coast, he began to hang around a boat rental operation. The owner, a man named Archie Borthwick, took him under his wing and encouraged him as he tinkered with boat motors. My father knew perfectly well that this was something he could not do for his son himself. Although there was something poignant in that realization, he was also able to acknowledge that in Archie my brother had found a kind of surrogate father. At the very least, it could be said that my brother had entered into an informal apprenticeship. Archie had helped to set him on a course that would develop his natural gifts and influence his choice of career.

This sort of mentorship can be found in many societies. Other men in the community initiate boys into aspects of adulthood in ways that the boys' fathers are not able to do; women often perform a similar function for girls. And although there are things that only a woman can teach a girl or only a man can teach a boy, there are also learnings that can cross gender lines.

In the course of our schooling, some of us have been lucky enough to encounter a teacher—of our own sex or the opposite—who has touched a chord and influenced us in a far-reaching way. One such teacher for me was my homeroom teacher in Grade 8, Marjorie Colpitts. She detected some nascent abilities in me and encouraged me to develop them.

A few years ago, having heard that Miss Colpitts was suffering from a terminal illness, I visited her in the hospital. My summer vacation was about to begin, and as I sat at her bedside it occurred to me that she would likely not survive until I returned to the city. As we talked I thought to myself, "What do I say to someone who has had such a positive influence on my life?" Sensing that this was the last opportunity I would have to tell her what she had done for me, I felt moved to say, "I want to thank you for believing in me."

This sense that we are following a trail that has been blazed for us by others has been experienced from time immemorial. The scriptures are full of examples of people whose way has been illuminated by their elders. The Old Testament prophet Jeremiah not only looked to his scribe, Baruch, to write down some of his oracles, but encouraged Baruch to imitate his master in staking his life on loyalty to God rather than on the lost cause of the dying kingdom of Judah (Jeremiah 45). Not only was Ruth schooled in the Hebrew faith by the teaching of her mother-in-law, Naomi; the older woman went on to coach her widowed daughter-in-law to meet her need for security by attracting the attention of a prospective new husband after they returned to

Bethlehem (Ruth 3:1–5). Another leading figure in the Hebrew scriptures, Elijah, took on a protege named Elisha. When the prophet was transported to heaven in a whirlwind, it was to Elisha that he passed on his mantle, the symbol of his authority (2 Kings 2:11–13).

In the New Testament, the apostle Paul's second letter to Timothy traces the influence of faith through three generations of a single family: "I am reminded of your sincere faith, a faith that lived first in your grandmother Lois and your mother Eunice and now, I am sure, lives in you" (2 Timothy 1:5). Another mentoring relationship is involved here as well: Paul himself has been teaching Timothy what it means to be a pastor. The disciples who called Jesus "Master" or "Teacher" thereby honoured him as a mentor. And the writer of the Letter to the Hebrews uses an image of Jesus as a trailblazer, calling him "the pioneer and perfecter of our faith" (Hebrews 12:2).

The dynamics of mentoring are not always as clear or intentional as these biblical examples might suggest. During a discussion of this subject in the men's spirituality group at my church, we realized that we were not always aware of it at the time when someone acted as our mentor. Sometimes these relationships can be less formal than those between a parent and a child, a teacher and a student, or a master and an apprentice. The real nature of an informal relationship may be recognized only in retrospect.

Nor are mentoring relationships always smooth. In fact, there are count-less examples of mentorships that have ended badly. In fields such as psycho-analysis and religious movements—to name two—there is no shortage of cases of disciples eventually chafing under the mentor's efforts to exercise control. Often the junior person in the relationship feels a need to break free, to leave the path the trailblazer has charted, and to step out on his or her own. When a mentor is unable to let go and allow that natural progression to happen, there can be a painful break in the relationship. Successful trailblazing requires a significant degree of grace and wisdom on the part of the mentor.

Trailblazers and Times of Crisis

In *The Lion, the Witch and the Wardrobe*—a volume of the popular *Chronicles of Narnia*—C.S. Lewis describes the predicament of four siblings who decide to go in search of a faun named Mr. Tumnus, but have no idea which way to go. Toward the end of the chapter titled "Into the Forest," a robin appears and looks at them intently. Lucy, the youngest, asks the bird to take them to the faun. By way of reply, the robin moves away, but only as far as the next tree. Lucy realizes that they are meant to follow. So the children follow as the bird—who obviously knows these woods—leads them from tree to tree, keeping in sight of them. Only when this phase of their journey is over does the robin disappear.

The children's experience illustrates a form of trailblazing—which may not always be recognized as such—relating to specific life episodes. In our formative years, we may need the guidance of more experienced people as we choose a career or develop values and convictions to live by. But there may also be particular periods when we face a challenge and need to know that others have been this way before and know the territory, that others have faced this issue and lived to tell the tale. In times of crisis or transition, I have benefited myself from the wisdom of those who had undergone similar experiences and had not been crushed by them. Other people can provide an assurance that, even though life might not feel very good at the moment, there is a fair chance that it will get better in the future.

I once knew a woman who had undergone a mastectomy, thereby learning first-hand of the fears, anxieties, and uncertainties that can attend that experience. Once she had recovered sufficiently, she decided to volunteer at the local cancer hospital. She met with women and their partners to speak of her own experience and to answer some of their questions. As a "wounded healer," she could fill a need that the health care professionals, for all their expertise, often could not. For many women over the years, she became the one who had gone ahead and blazed the trail that made it a little easier for those who came after.

Similarly, people who gather in support groups do so to meet a shared need. Organizations like Alcoholics Anonymous, grief recovery groups, or coming-out groups for gay men and lesbians typically provide opportunities for those who are further along in the experience—perhaps just a tree or two ahead along the trail—to tell their stories. Those who are newer to the experience gain a sense of what they might expect. They can be helped to avoid some of the pitfalls along the path. And above all, they are offered the priceless gift of hope.

As the dynamics of a support group illustrate, trailblazing can be an ongoing process. Many groups of this kind are designed to meet a particular need at a particular stage in a person's life. A group member may begin the process with a strong need to receive what more experienced group members have to offer. In time, the balance begins to shift. The person who was once so new to it all becomes a kind of elder who has wisdom to offer those who have come behind.

In time, individuals may pass out of the group altogether, but having gained an understanding that can be passed on to others in less formal settings.

Mentoring may also come not from an individual but from a mentoring community. At critical moments, the beliefs and values that permeate the atmosphere of a summer camp, an educational institution, or a religious congregation can have a profound effect. The influence of a group of people and their way of looking at the world may not only provide what is needed at that particular juncture, but also affect the subsequent development of one's life.

Links in a Chain

As wisdom and experience, encouragement and guidance are passed on within a community or from one person to the next, the image of links in a chain comes to mind. Given time, we who have been helped by those who are somewhere ahead of us on the path will find an opportunity (as a movie title puts it) to "pay it forward." Passing on the things we have experienced and assuring others that they too will survive repays some of the debt owed to those who have encouraged us.

The image of links in a chain can also describe larger spiritual issues of mentorship, like discerning a vocation or passing on a belief system. A church where I was once minister invited a senator and former Moderator of The United Church of Canada, the Very Rev. Lois Wilson, to be guest preacher for the congregation's centenary. In introducing this small but fiery spiritual leader to the gathering, I mentioned that my father had a book that had been given to him when he had spoken many years earlier at a Student Christian Movement conference. Among the university students who had signed the book had been Lois Freeman, later to become Lois Wilson. When she came to the microphone, our guest preacher put me in my place as only Lois Wilson can do. She said that she had indeed learned from my father, but that he had learned from *her* father, who had been dean of the Faculty of Theology that my father had attended as a student. "And now, Clark," she said, "you're sitting here learning from me." From her father to my father to her to me: the connections were indeed like links in a chain.

Sometimes we may acquire physical objects that symbolize more than themselves. They are associated with particular people, very often the ones who have influenced us in some way. We may even think of those objects as a kind of trust to be passed on to those who come after.

I think of a hundred-year-old piano that has been in my family for most of its existence. My grandparents bought it second-hand when my mother and her sister were girls so that they could take piano lessons. My brothers and I practised our lessons on that same piano, and now my daughter enjoys sitting down from time to time to play it. I still recall some favourite pieces that my mother played years ago on this instrument—an instrument on which her granddaughter continues to make music. And because my mother's values affected me and her encouragement sustained me, I am glad that this tangible reminder of her is still in the family. It is a physical link to the generation before me and to those that will follow. It helps to meet my spiritual need for a sense of belonging, connection, and continuity.

Perhaps you can trace the story of a significant object that has come to you or that you have passed on to someone else. In my own family, I could add such examples as a 175-year-old grandfather clock, a baptismal gown, a signet ring, or a heartfelt letter. There can be added significance when such an object connects you to a namesake. For example, I am glad to own a wristwatch that belonged to the grandfather for whom I am named. That he and I were very close when I was a boy makes the significance all the sweeter. He introduced me to some interests that I continue to explore 40 years after his death, and I count him among my own trailblazers.

Of course, not all objects with symbolic value are handed down through the family; some come from friends or other influences. Nor do we necessarily hang on for a long time to the items that come to us. When my younger brother was facing surgery for cancer, a woman gave him a "prayer stone" that had been presented to her when she was a cancer patient herself. But the stone was clearly not his to keep. In due time it was to be passed on to others who, like those before them, would hold it in their hands as they used it to help focus their prayers.

Thoughts about the people who have influenced your life—who have helped to lead the way as you developed your interests, chose your career path, adopted a set of values, or tried to find your way through a challenging time—may inspire feelings of gratitude. But what can you do with these feelings? One obvious thing is to say thank you. I was glad of an opportunity to say thank you to Miss Colpitts for her confidence and encouragement when I had been her student.

When I heard that one of my trailblazers was about to retire, I saw it as an opportunity to write him a letter of appreciation. I remember quoting in my letter what a Scottish educator, Principal John Cairns, wrote long ago to his teacher, Sir William Hamilton. Whatever still lay before him, he wrote, he would always bear the mark of his teacher.

Trailblazers are sometimes surprised to discover the influence they have had. You may have experienced that sense of surprise when someone has thanked you for blazing a trail for him or her. Knowing how good it feels when people tell you about something you were able to give them—an encouraging word that they took to heart, or a piece of advice that saved them from making a serious mistake—you may be encouraged to express your appreciation to people who have done such things for you. In saying thank you, you will strengthen a bond with that other person and, in the process, help to meet the need of both of your spirits for a sense of connection and significance.

If one thing you can do with a feeling of gratitude to your trailblazers is to express it to them, the other is to pass on to others the things your trailblazers have given—things that may have been refined further in the crucible of your own experience. Some of us have been able to respond to a request to be a mentor in a specific aspect of someone's work or life. But other, less formal mentorships are constantly taking form as you make your wisdom, your reflections on lived experience, your encouragement, and your hope available to other people. In so many ways, life constantly provides you with opportunities to blaze a trail for others as they try to find their way through the woods.

For personal reflection or group discussion

1. Among those who have been trailblazers for you, can you think of one whose trailblazing role was clear to you at the time and another whose role you realized only in retrospect?

2. Not including relatives, has anyone of the opposite sex played the role of trailblazer for you? Has the difference in gender brought anything distinctive to the mentoring relationship?

3. Have you gone through a particularly challenging time in your life in which an individual or group of people who have gone through a similar experience has been able to help guide your footsteps? Have you found ways to express your appreciation or to "pay it forward"?

4. Can you think of a time when you have acted as a trailblazer for someone else?

chapter 2

forbidden fruit
the woods and the loss of innocence

When I was still young and relatively innocent, I took a walk in a local park. As I passed a small wooded area, I heard a strange combination of sounds—a murmur of voices, a rustling of leaves—coming from somewhere among the trees. Feeling curious but cautious, I ventured into the woods until I could see the source of the sounds. A young couple were lying among the leaves having sex. It was a discovery that I found strange and fascinating, exciting and disturbing. I felt somewhat like the Little Red Ridinghood character in the Sondheim/Lapine musical *Into the Woods*, who records that her sexually charged encounter with the Big Bad Wolf left her feeling "excited—well, excited and scared."[1] A fear of being discovered, together with my sense of propriety, led me to leave this illicit scene.

IN THINKING BACK on that encounter in the woods, I am reminded of another lyric from a musical. In "Typically English" from *Stop the World: I Want to Get Off*, a young woman sings of her mother's warning to stay away from the woods and from playing with young men there. Then the young woman describes her "naughty" urge to disobey.

The forest can be a fearful place, in both fairy tales and real life. To begin, the forest evokes parental fears for the safety of a child. Certainly it represents a place where children might wander beyond their parents' control or protection. And many a parent's worst nightmare is the possibility that a child will be abducted, harmed, and perhaps even killed. In connection with this, a forest brings to mind a place of danger. Too many missing persons—children and adults—eventually turn up in shallow graves in wooded areas.

But the mother's prohibition in that little song is based on a less extreme fear. It may simply reflect the anxiety that a parent feels as a child grows up.

Why does the young woman's mother tell her particularly to avoid the young men in the woods? Perhaps out of a parent's protective impulses. She may fear an unwanted pregnancy, or an experience that will leave her daughter feeling hurt. On the other hand, through a sexual entanglement, someone other than the mother could become primary in the daughter's life. The forest is a place where her daughter may, in one way or another, become lost to her. For the daughter, the discoveries that she will make and the knowledge that she will acquire will rob her of the innocence of childhood. For the mother, the steps the child is taking toward adulthood will threaten the closeness of the mother–daughter relationship.

In the song, a warning is given, but also disobeyed. Such disobedience is often a feature of stories about children going into the woods—whether in fairy tales or in more modern stories. For example, when the storybook *Franklin Is Lost* introduces a prohibition on the first page—Franklin is a turtle who is "not allowed to go into the woods alone"[2]—the reader knows instinctively that there will be no story unless the prohibition is disobeyed.

East of Eden

The Judeo-Christian scriptures, too, begin with just such a story. The second creation story in Genesis recounts a story of a prohibition, an act of disobedience, and the consequent acquisition of knowledge and loss of innocence. The story of Adam and Eve is set in a garden rather than a forest, but the garden has "every tree that is pleasant to the sight and good for food, the tree of life also in the midst of the garden, and the tree of the knowledge of good and evil" (Genesis 2:9).

The prohibition forbids eating the fruit of this last tree. Even if this were an unfamiliar story, one could well anticipate that this rule is bound to be broken. When it is, the couple—who had previously been unaware of their naked-ness—suddenly have their eyes opened and sense a need to cover themselves. The suggestion, some say, is that in eating the fruit of the tree the human beings have appropriated to themselves (and taken from God) the right to decide what is good and what is evil. As the story is told, their disobedience results in a Fall from a state of innocence and their expulsion from the wooded garden. Life will now become harder for them. But perhaps the hardest thing of all will be a sense of alienation from God.

As with other stories in which the characters seem almost "set up" by some-thing forbidden—whether the taboo is against going into the woods, eating forbidden fruit, or opening a Pandora's box—there is a sense of inevitabil-ity about the events that unfold. There are "good" things that cannot happen unless this apparently "bad" thing happens first. If we are to move toward spiri-tual maturity, innocence is bound to be lost sooner or later, knowledge (sexual and otherwise) is bound to be acquired, and lessons are bound to be learned.

This mysterious paradox was explored in a 15th-century carol that is sung during the Advent and Christmas seasons. Called "Adam Lay Y-bounden," it unfolds the mystery this way:

Adam lay y-bounden,
Bounden in a bond;
Four thousand winter
Thought he not too long;
And all was for an apple
An apple that he took
As clerkes finden written
In theire book.
Ne had the apple taken been,
The apple taken been,
Ne hadde never Lady
A been heaven's queen.
Blessed be the time

That apple taken was!
Therefore we may singen
Deo Gratias![3]

In what today seems a strange kind of logic, the songwriter suggests that if Adam had never eaten the apple, there would have been no Fall, and if there had been no Fall, there would have been no need for redemption. Hence, there would have been no need for a redeemer (Christ) or the Lady (Mary) to give birth to him. In short, without the disobedience of eating the apple, Mary would never have become the Queen of Heaven. And because the writer is convinced that it is a good thing for Mary to be Queen of Heaven, he can say, "Blessed be the time / That apple taken was!"

Whether or not this convoluted reasoning speaks to us, we know from experience that acquiring knowledge and losing a certain kind of innocence are part of growing up—and that a loss of innocence can be painful. Often we acquire knowledge about the way things are in the "real world"—or at least in the adult world—in a way that brings a kind of disillusionment. A child suddenly realizes where the meat on the dinner table comes from. An adolescent catches an admired adult in a lie. A teenager gradually discovers that a parent is more complex (and perhaps less honourable) than she had imagined. These are all experiences that can leave people feeling sadder and wiser—and perhaps less confident about their perceptions.

In the contrasting collections of poems *Songs of Innocence* and *Songs of Experience*, William Blake evokes images of childlike simplicity on the one hand and visions of a more puzzling, complex, and uncontained world on the other. Taking a lamb as an image of innocence, he asks the little lamb who its maker is, and answers with an allusion to Christ, also referred to as a lamb. The best-known of the *Songs of Experience*, a poem called "The Tyger," asks a question, too. After listing some characteristics of this less benign creature, Blake asks whether the tiger's maker is the same as the lamb's. This rhetorical question, unlike the one about who made the lamb, is left unanswered. But it is a question that the voice of experience cannot avoid asking.

The Necessity of Disillusionment

A 1970s movie called *Breaking Away* has become something of a cult favourite. A teenaged boy—the central character in this coming-of-age story—is critical of the dishonest business practices in which his father engages. But he admires an Italian cycling team that is coming to town and sets out to race with them. When he shows that he can keep up with them, one of the Italian cyclists jams a stick between his spokes, sending him into a ditch. Dragging himself home, the boy is both shattered by his disillusionment and embarrassed at what now seems his naïveté. The lesson he's learned, he says sadly, is that "everybody cheats." He just hadn't known.

Discovering that people we admire have feet of clay can be an experience that brings a disillusioning loss of innocence. Nathaniel Hawthorne's short story "Young Goodman Brown," set in the context of the Salem witch trials, explores the idea that things are not always what they seem.

Hawthorne sets the story in a forest. Young Goodman Brown says goodbye to his wife and goes into the woods. A mysterious, sinister stranger joins him as a guide and reveals that a number of people he knows and admires—including members of his family, his minister, and the catechism teacher who is still his spiritual adviser—are actually sinners who worship the devil. A dreamlike sequence of events brings him to a ceremony in the middle of the forest where he rejoins his wife. The two of them are to be initiated into some evil cult. Like a latter-day Adam and Eve, they are described as "the only pair, as it seemed, who were yet hesitating on the verge of wickedness in this dark world."[4]

At the climactic moment, the scene dissolves and Goodman Brown finds himself back on the streets of Salem village. But the experience—dream or not—has robbed him of his illusions. After having encountered his neighbours in the wild setting of the woods, he looks on them with new, jaded eyes.

The story is a haunting one, extreme in its suggestion that people who appear to be good are in fact evil. In reality, most people are at neither one end of the spectrum nor the other. But in the experiences through which we lose our innocence about others, we often discover that they are more complex and less benevolent than we had imagined.

We emerge from such experiences feeling disillusioned—without illusions. And that, in a sense, is a good thing. It is not good to base our lives on misperceptions about people or about human nature. But after an illusion is gone, the challenge is to not become cynical or unduly suspicious. In the movie *Romanoff and Juliet*, a satire on the Cold War, one character accuses another of being a pessimist. But the other objects. He is an optimist, he says, because he knows what a terrible place the world can be. His accuser is the pessimist, because he is forever finding out.

What is the opposite of innocence? According to one understanding of the word, its opposite would be guilt. But I would suggest that its opposite—or at least its desired opposite—is spiritual maturity. And that means not vacillating wildly between naive and cynical attitudes toward people, but achieving a degree of balance in which one expects from people neither the very best nor the very worst.

The Truth about Ourselves

The journey toward maturity includes a loss of innocence about ourselves, as well. This chapter began with an image of sexuality as a kind of knowledge that brings with it a loss of innocence. But just as discovering the role that sexuality plays can challenge a child's assumptions about human life, a growing awareness of our own sexuality can challenge our assumptions about ourselves. How often has it happened that someone who was regarded as a "nice girl" or a "nice boy" (and who regarded herself or himself in this way) enters adolescence and begins to have fantasies that challenge this image? What sort of nice girl or boy has thoughts like these—reducing people to objects, perhaps feeling aggressive or even predatory?

The challenge, of course, is integrating this new element of self-awareness into our personalities so that we can become healthy and mature adults. And not all of us are entirely successful in undertaking this process. But the task of coming to terms with our own sexuality parallels other kinds of self-discovery and personal growth that are necessary as our innocence about ourselves is lost.

When the boy in *Breaking Away* says "everybody cheats," one may wonder whether he includes himself in that statement. Is he also feeling disillusioned about himself? Hard as it is to face the truth about other people, it can be even harder to face the truth about ourselves. Think about the times when you have felt let down by someone: the colleague who had been gossiping behind your back, the spouse who may have betrayed you, the friend who seemed to forget all about you in your hour of need. In experiences like these, people inevitably see the issue from their own point of view. You may be justified in feeling hurt, disappointed, or angry. But what may be more difficult to see is whether your own behaviour has been less than exemplary. Is there a way in which you may have contributed to this situation? Are you entirely without fault?

Some of us can recognize times in our lives when we have been disappointed in ourselves, times when we have let ourselves down. You may have lashed out in a way that you could never have imagined yourself doing. You may have nursed bitter, vengeful thoughts. You may have experienced what in German is called *schadenfreude*—a nasty kind of satisfaction that takes pleasure in the suffering of an adversary. If you paused and looked at yourself at these times, you may not have liked what you saw. Your own self-image may have been damaged. In fact, you may have been unpleasantly surprised to find that you were capable of feelings and actions that you would certainly not condone in someone else.

It is one thing to lose your innocence with regard to your opinion of other people, but it is quite another to lose your innocence about yourself. And yet, when the apostle Paul expressed his understanding of this, he did not say, "Other people have sinned and fall short of the glory of God." His honesty about himself led him to say, "*All* have sinned and fall short of the glory of God" (Romans 3:23). And he no doubt included himself in that statement.

If spiritual maturity requires coming to a balanced understanding of other people and of humanity in general, it also requires coming to a balanced understanding of ourselves. That means being neither a self-deprecating person who can affirm nothing positive in herself or himself, nor the sort of self-involved person who cannot conceive of the possibility of being wrong. It means freeing yourself from the illusion that you are either better or worse than everyone else and from the illusion that there can be no legitimate perspective other than your own. It means being sufficiently "centred" in your life not to be thrown off balance by every new discovery about others or about yourself. It means achieving a state of mind and soul in which you have learned some of the harder lessons of life and have emerged, not unscathed, but with a deepened appreciation of the human condition and a deepened self-understanding.

For personal reflection or group discussion

1. Can you recall a time in your childhood or youth when you had an experience of disillusionment or loss of innocence about someone in your life? How did that discovery feel?

2. Can you think of a way in which a loss of innocence was necessary for you to lose some unhelpful illusions and acquire a degree of spiritual maturity?

3. Have you ever been disappointed in yourself and in the way you reacted to an event in your life? Did this experience affect the way you understand yourself?

chapter 3

two roads diverge
forks in the path

In the famous poem "The Road Not Taken," Robert Frost describes two roads diverging in a yellow wood. I was reminded of Frost's experience when the path I was following through a forest, after it wound for some distance without revealing any unusual geographical features, brought me face to face with an enormous boulder, deposited there in some prehistoric glacial age. The path divided at that point. I could choose between making a 90 degree turn to my right or a 90 degree turn to my left. There was little to choose between the two; like the forking path in Frost's poem, they were each worn about the same. Which way should I go?

FACED WITH A CHOICE OF PATHS, you may not glean much help from the advice ascribed to Yogi Berra: "When you come to a fork in the road, take it." Frost puts the dilemma well when he points out that no one traveller could follow both of the routes before him or her. To take both paths at once would be as impossible as to be in two places at the same time. When you come to a fork in the road, you simply have to choose which way to go.

Umberto Eco describes a metaphor of Jorge Luis Borges in which a wood is represented as "a garden of forking paths. Even when there are no well-trodden paths in a wood, everyone can trace his or her own path, deciding to go to the left or to the right of a certain tree and making a choice at every tree encountered."[1] As this image suggests, we make more choices in life than we realize.

Looking back over the course of your life, what were some of the major forks in the road? Did you sense, at these junctures, that you had a choice to make?

Young adulthood is a period in which people often find themselves coming to one fork in the road after another. Which educational route should I follow? Which career path should I pursue? With which person should I become romantically involved? If I take a certain path, what other paths will become closed to me?

Sometimes the choice of path is easy. You may be presented with several possibilities, but one choice clearly makes the best use of your gifts, offers the best opportunity for personal fulfillment, or leads to the most faithful expression of your values and convictions. At other times, a sense of clarity can come from realizing that choices you have already made have set your life in a particular direction.

I once knew a woman who, in her younger days, had been a professional singer in a prairie city. In her 20s, she had won a competition that could have opened up a career with the Metropolitan Opera in New York. But she was slightly older than most of the other competitors. She was already married and had very young children. On reflection, it seemed to her that she had already made her choice—she did not want the kind of career that would require her to spend so much time away from her family. She chose instead to do occasional work as a soloist in the small city where she lived, creating a larger space in her life for raising her children. Although she may sometimes have wondered about the road not taken, she had no real regrets about this choice.

Other choices of which path to take can be much harder. Two different career opportunities may be equally appealing. A choice between staying where you are and moving to another town may prompt you to make a list of pros and cons, only to find that the lists are roughly the same length. You may find that one path appeals to your head—the rational, responsible side of your nature—while the other appeals to your heart—the part that is willing to take risks for the sake of a deeper sense of fulfillment. Your own particular personality may ultimately lead you to lean in one direction or the other. Or you may find yourself waiting things out, hoping perhaps that one of the paths will be eliminated and you will be left with only one way to go through the woods.

A Matter of Choice?

This raises the question of how much choice you really have when it comes to deciding whether to go, as Borges puts it, "to the left or to the right of a certain tree." In one sense, you may have less choice than you often imagine. But as we will discuss later, in another sense, more paths may be open than you realize.

At many forks in the road, the path has already been chosen for you. Sometimes it has been chosen by other people.

Think of the forks in the road that you encountered as a child. How often was the path chosen for you by adults? When you were very young, decisions about which extracurricular activities you participated in, where you lived, and whether or not you attended a church or other community organizations were all decisions which—although you might have had some input—your parents would make. And from the path that was chosen, others followed. Some of us may have had a parent who was transferred to another city by an employer. That decision was made by adults, but it would affect childhood friendships, schools, influences, and so on.

Even as adults, there are times when the choice of path is largely controlled by other people. When I was a young minister serving my first church, a number of acquaintances urged me to apply for a vacant position at our denomination's head office. These people knew me through a national church committee I had served on. They had the ear of the search committee and led me to believe that I was a shoe-in for the job.

At first, I was reluctant to apply. It would have meant moving to a big city where my wife knew no one. We were just starting a family, and it would have involved a good deal of travel and time away from home. Yet I was persuaded that I had something to offer and that this was an opportunity I should not miss. With a fair degree of confidence, I accepted an invitation to an interview.

But the interview did not go well. The next day I received a phone call from the chair of the search committee telling me that they had decided not to offer me the position.

This episode has taken on a particular meaning in my personal mythology. It was one of my first significant experiences of failure, and I know that dealing with failure has a part to play in becoming a mature human being. But it also illustrates that paths are not always ours to choose. I made a choice in agreeing to apply for the position. But the decision about whether that path would ultimately become open to me rested with others.

People sometimes speak of personal relationships—with a life partner or with a friend—as if decisions about them lie entirely with one person. But just as it takes two to tango, it takes both parties to begin and to continue a relationship. One spouse's desire to maintain a marriage might be thwarted by the other spouse's decision to end it. A child may want to make friends with another, but find his or her overtures rejected. A couple might put a lot of energy into keeping a friendship going with another couple but receive little encouragement in return. They begin to get the message that this friendship has become a one-way street, or that somewhere along the way, they must have come to a fork in the road and the other couple took a different turn. We are not always as free as we imagine to choose which path to follow—or who will accompany us on that path. Other people's choices may play a decisive part.

Sometimes it is circumstances that incline a person toward one fork or another. For some people, a range of available choices may be determined by socio-economic status, race, or sex, or limited by disability or chronic illness. For others, the circumstances of a particular period in their lives may play a decisive part.

When he was discharged from the army at the end of the Second World War, my father explored a number of career options. It was his second choice that came through with an offer first. The day after my father accepted this position, he received a telegram offering him the job he would have preferred. But he had already agreed to the first offer, and he felt that he could not go back on his word. Timing and circumstance had played a part in the path he would take.

Events can intervene and close a path that you had planned to pursue. As a girl, a woman I came to know in her old age had been planning to attend a prestigious high school on a scholarship, when her father died unexpectedly and she had to get a job to help support her family. Her formal education suddenly came to an end. A retired couple I once knew had planned a relaxed retirement, but circumstances intervened. Their daughter, a single parent, reached a point where she was unable to care for her two young sons. In their 70s, this couple found themselves raising two energetic school-aged boys. The carefree retirement they had anticipated did not materialize.

When circumstances or other people's decisions affect—or even dictate—your path, it is a reminder that you are not always completely free to choose when you come to a crossroads. At other times, though, more options may be available than you realize.

When you face a dilemma, a friend or a counsellor might ask whether you have considered a certain course of action. "Oh, no," you might say, "I could never do that." Perhaps to do a certain thing would be out of character and contrary to your values. The opera singer could have joined the Met and moved to New York. But her desire not to sacrifice her family life meant that such a path was not really open to her. My father could have reneged on his agreement to take the first job that was offered him in order to pursue the option that appealed to him more. But for him, his word was his bond, and he did not have it in him to get out of the commitment he had made.

It is good to know that you have a bottom line. When a path is appealing but would involve stooping to behaviour that would call your sense of self into question, it is good to know that this is not a path that you could really pursue. But at other times, a branch of a path may be a good one to follow, but your experience of life has not yet brought you to a point where you can seriously consider it.

Some people may be unable to conceive of leaving a destructive relationship because they cannot imagine life on their own or cannot see a way of making such a life financially viable. Others might not be able to consider a career change in mid-life because they are uncomfortable with that degree of risk or because a sense of responsibility to the people who depend on them stands in the way. A person may be assigned by her siblings the role of caregiver for an aging parent. There are other options, other ways of meeting the need, but she cannot see them.

At various forks in the path of life there may be, in theory, any number of possible choices. But in practice, what others regard as viable options are not always available to you. You may be able to consider such a path sometime. In fact, it might be good for you to move toward such a point. But you cannot do it now. You just don't have it in you. Or, as a woman I know often puts it, it isn't in your repertoire.

A Family's Experience with Diverging Roads

How much freedom do we have to choose? When is the path we take influenced by circumstances or by decisions made by others? What limits do our personalities or upbringing place on the options that we are able to recognize? All of these factors come into play in the story of a family that is recounted in the opening chapter of the Book of Ruth in the Hebrew scriptures.

The story begins with a woman from Bethlehem named Naomi and her household. At a time of famine in their homeland, this Hebrew family moves to the neighbouring Gentile country of Moab. Naomi's two sons grow up to marry Moabite women named Orpah and Ruth. In time, Naomi's husband and her two sons die, leaving three widows. Times have improved back home, so Naomi decides to return to Bethlehem. Her daughters-in-law have grown so attached to her that they insist on going with her to this unknown country. Naomi tries to reason with them. Without Hebrew husbands, they will have no status among the people of Bethlehem. Eventually, with many tears from all three women, Orpah agrees to stay with her own people. But Ruth insists on accompanying Naomi back to the older woman's homeland.

This story, though briefly told, is full of forks in the road, and at every turn a distinct set of dynamics comes into play. It begins with a move that seems to be decided by circumstances. To Naomi and her husband, staying at Bethlehem in a time of famine would hardly have been an option. The land of Moab was their closest friendly neighbour, so it may have been an obvious choice to go there. Their two sons—and in their culture it might not have mattered how old they were—were obliged to fall in with a decision that was made by their parents, a decision that would affect the subsequent course of their lives.

The next crossroads that Naomi came to in her life was, similarly, not one that she came to willingly or over which she had much control. The deaths of all three men in the family presented her with another decision about where to live. Once again the choice seemed obvious. Not that it was an easy decision; she had formed a close attachment to Orpah and Ruth, and the thought of leaving them was painful. But just as their position in Hebrew society would have been insecure without a man's protection, Naomi's position in Moab would have been uncertain, too. In any case, the decision that Naomi made was affected by changed circumstances. Conditions back in Bethlehem had improved. No doubt that made going home appear to be the sensible choice.

Now it was the turn of Orpah and Ruth to make a decision about which path to follow. In the end they made different choices. This in itself suggests a greater degree of freedom to choose than at some of the other junctures. Orpah, persuaded by Naomi's argument, decided to remain in Moab. Ruth, however, insisted on going with Naomi. But how can we account for the different paths each woman chose at this parting of the ways?

Was Orpah the kind of person who was inclined to choose with her head, while Ruth was more likely to be ruled by her heart? Did Orpah find comfort in the familiar, while Ruth was more inclined to take risks and more open to the possibility of adventure? Was there something in their personalities or their upbringing that provided them with different "repertoires" as they came to this moment?

"Orpah kissed her mother-in-law [goodbye]," we're told, "but Ruth clung to her" (Ruth 1:14). Both women were close to Naomi—but was Ruth's attachment more compelling? The story passes no judgment on Orpah for her decision to stay with her own people. Such a choice would certainly have been understandable to the writer and to those who first heard this story. The moment of parting is a particularly poignant one. It underscores the pain and difficulty the women experienced when confronted with a hard choice.

The consequences of Orpah's decision for herself are not part of the story; Orpah disappears from the narrative. The action follows Ruth as she returns to Bethlehem with Naomi. Ruth's choice, however reckless and impractical it may have seemed, is vindicated. She ends up marrying a kinsman of Naomi's husband, a man named Boaz. She raises a family and acquires a respected name among Naomi's people. King David would be among her great-grand-children.

The Paths Not Taken

Did Ruth ever wonder how different her life would have been if she had stayed in Moab? Did Orpah ever gaze wistfully westward and consider what would have become of her if she had gone with the other women? Did either of them have cause to feel regret or relief?

Inevitably as we go through life's forest, we come to major and minor forks in the road. And when a path is chosen—whether by ourselves, by other people, by chance or circumstance, or by a combination of these elements—other routes are left unexplored. To choose one thing is often, in a sense, to sacrifice another. How do you feel about the paths you have not taken? In his poem, Frost speaks of keeping the road not taken for another day. But recognizing that one way tends to lead on to another, he doubts whether he would ever actually retrace his steps to that fork to see where the other path might have led.

How do you feel about the paths you might have taken but did not? Do you feel regret? Or do you have a sense that, on the whole, your life has turned out as it was meant to? Your degree of comfort with things as they are may depend in part on how much say you feel you had. You may feel resentful if some promising paths were closed by the decisions of others.

Some years ago I was involved with a group of people who had recently come through an experience of separation or divorce. Each of us was embarking on a new branch in the path, a new stage in our lives. The word "divorce" comes from the Latin *divortium*, meaning a fork in a road or a river. And we knew from experience not only that we had come to a parting of the ways, but that we were in new territory. But as much as we had in common, there were significant differences among us, and because of those differences, the group foundered.

The essential difference, it seemed to me, was the degree of participation each of us felt we had had in creating the situation in which we found ourselves. Some of us felt that we were at least 50 percent responsible for choosing to end the relationship and embark on a new path. Others, though, had been blindsided by a spouse who had unilaterally decided that the marriage was over. The issues of these members of the group were vastly different from the issues faced by those who had actively participated in the decision. Those who felt that they had been sent down a path that was not of their choosing were, understandably, resentful.

Yet sometimes, it must be admitted, an event that seemed like a disaster at the time may appear in a more positive light when seen from a greater distance. When Winston Churchill's Conservative Party lost the first general election after the Second World War, Churchill felt the sting of rejection by the British people. His wife, Clementine, tried to comfort him by suggesting that this loss might be a blessing in disguise. If so, he replied, it was quite effectively disguised. And yet, when the path that would have led him to form another government was closed, he was offered a path that allowed him time to do some of his most significant writing. That God never closes a door without opening a window may be a cliché, but like most clichés it has a kernel of truth in it.

A year after the disappointment of not being offered the job at our church's head office, a golden opportunity came to me that used my gifts and suited my stage of life far better. I was called to a growing suburban congregation where my family felt very much at home, reminding me that it was in parish ministry that I really belonged. With hindsight I came to feel that, had I been allowed to pursue that other path, I would have found myself in a difficult situation for me and for the people I cared about. From a greater distance, the decision that had disappointed me looked like a narrow escape. How often I have thought of the words of an nonagenarian I once knew: "If you can't be grateful for what you've had, then at least be grateful for what you've been spared!"

Our feelings as we look back at some of the roads not taken may also depend on whether those roads seem closed forever. Is it true that opportunity only knocks once? When it comes to a particular opportunity—a job, a relationship, a move—it may well be. Some of the paths we might consider depend on a unique coincidence of a variety of factors. Some options may only be open to us at certain stages of life. But some people who have passed by one vocation in favour of another find ways to incorporate that other path by claiming it as an avocation.

I was on my way to becoming a university history teacher when a variety of factors intervened and I felt led into ministry. And yet in my chosen work, I have found room for teaching. The part of me that likes to teach adults still finds scope for expression. The woman who had been a promising young singer may have had moments of wistfulness as she thought of the "might-have-beens" of an opera career. But she made a life for herself that honoured the other things that were important to her and still included some use of her talents as a singer.

Some people had to reject a path that appealed to them in their youth because the thing they loved did not offer a viable way of making a living. And yet that other path may be explored as a sideline. A business person continues to play the sport at which she excels. A carpenter forms a rock group in mid-life and returns to playing the music of his youth. A magazine editor writes murder mysteries in his spare time. Some people find a way through the woods that combines a major and a minor path.

Beckoning Trails

An anthology of stories, essays, and poems that was widely used by an earlier generation of schoolchildren bore the title *Beckoning Trails*. Some of the forks that you come to in life may present two or more options, but neither is more compelling than the other. At other points in the journey, though, you may feel that a particular trail is beckoning.

People who regard their life's work as a vocation feel that way about it. The word "vocation," of course, comes from the Latin *vocare*, meaning to call. The English mezzo-soprano Janet Baker once said that she was born to sing. The need to sing laid claim to her life as nothing else did. She could probably relate to people who say about their career—or about some other aspect of their life—that they didn't choose the path, the path chose them.

Another sense in which you may experience a particular trail beckoning is in the way you respond to a crisis. Many factors come into play. A person may respond to a life-threatening illness with courage, cheerfulness, and an openness to learning something through this experience, or by giving up and starting to die. As a man I once knew would often say after he had been diagnosed with a terminal illness, "We don't always get to choose the path we find ourselves on in life, but we do get to choose how we will navigate it." Personality, quality of relationships, experience of life to this point, and the physical toll the illness takes may all have a bearing on a person's response. But to the extent that you have the power to choose the nature of your response, you may feel drawn to a particular way of dealing with this challenge. One way may beckon more strongly than any other option.

You may also have a choice when it comes to responding to a conflict, an experience of rejection, or some other hurt or emotional wound. If it is possible to "take the high road," then presumably one could choose instead to take the low road. The low road might be the path that leads to speaking openly, harshly, and often about the people you believe have hurt you. This way leads to blame and bitterness. The high road—the road that leads you to lick your wounds and move on—may be the harder route to follow. But you may have sensed the loftier trail beckoning more strongly, and you may find yourself growing in stature as you follow it. The Book of Proverbs (15:24) says, "for the wise the path of life leads upward."

This chapter may have prompted you to review past episodes in your life. But what of the future? No one knows what the future holds. No one knows what circumstances beyond your control will influence the range of paths that will be opened—or closed—in the next stage of your life.

But as you look ahead, what are some of the forks in the road you expect to encounter in, say, the next five years? Will you need to make a decision about your career or about a particular job? Will you come to a crossroads in a significant relationship? Will you need to choose whether to retire or to keep on working? And if you do retire, whether to continue living in your community or to move somewhere else?

As you come to these forks in the road, what factors will influence the choices you make? Will your decisions be purely pragmatic? Will the needs of other people be a factor? Will your choices reflect a set of values that is consistent with the way you have lived your life to this point, or will they be based on another set of values?

For personal reflection or group discussion

1. Take a piece of paper and draw on it a road map of your life. Include some major forks in the road—points at which your life might have gone in one direction but went in another. Thinking about one of these junctures, how free were you to choose which route to take at that point? To what degree did other factors—circumstances or the influence of other people—affect the route your life followed?

2. Again considering one of the forks in the road on your map, have you ever wondered about how your life might have turned out differently if you had followed the other path? What words would you use to describe your wonderings (e.g., curious, wistful, resentful, relieved)? If that other path still appeals to you, is it too late to explore it?

3. What forks in the road do you expect to come to in the next few years? Review the questions posed in the last paragraphs of this chapter.

chapter 4

lost in the woods

going astray

Ashleigh Mitchell, a young woman I know, has spent a number of summers in Riding Mountain National Park in western Manitoba. One day, having heard of an old open-air church built in the woods by Mennonite conscientious objectors during the Second World War, she set out on her own to find it. She took a wrong turn, and made her way deep into the forest along an ancient trail of twists, turns, and forks. Eventually she realized that she had been following animal tracks, but by then she was thoroughly lost. Fear washed over her as she turned in circles of confusion. The trees appeared to stretch out identically in all directions, and thick clouds obliterated the sun. Gripped by terror and feeling out of control, she thrashed wildly through the bushes until at last she crossed a trail that looked like one of her original paths. Following this trail she finally found her way out of the forest. It was an experience that left her feeling grateful and relieved, but shaken.

EVERY YEAR, ESPECIALLY IN THE SUMMER, the news media carry reports of children or adults who have gotten lost in the woods. The story may end happily, with the one who was lost being found. Or, by the time searchers have found him or her, it may be too late—the person has not survived the hunger and thirst or the effects of the elements. Some who are lost find their own way out of the woods; others stay put to give themselves a better chance of being discovered. And some, through panic and disorientation, are driven around in circles on a desperate quest to get out of the bush.

We all know how it feels to be lost. You may have lost your way in the woods, driving somewhere unfamiliar, or walking through a large shopping mall. Tourists who visit the maze at Hampton Court in England make a game of trying to find their way out, although the game can be frustrating and even frightening at times. Frustration and fear are only two of the emotions associated with getting lost. You may become angry at yourself for not listening more carefully to directions or for letting yourself be separated from a companion. You may worry, not just for yourself, but for those who are anxiously looking for you. You may feel guilty for creating such anxiety; you may feel profoundly isolated and lonely. And just as these myriad feelings can be provoked by literal lostness, they can be responses to an experience of being lost in life.

When can you be overtaken by the sense of having lost your way? At any time, certainly. But particularly at certain life stages, such as young adulthood.

Young people who are faced with the need to choose an educational or career path often have difficulty negotiating the terrain. They may travel or enrol in a course partly to fill in time because they don't know which way to go. A young woman who had graduated with a university degree but didn't know what to do or where to go next described herself to me as "lost." The path she had been on didn't seem to be leading her anywhere. Or perhaps she had been following a path in a particular direction, but had strayed from it when its destination began to lose its appeal.

Mid-life can also produce a sense of lostness. Dante's *Divine Comedy* opens with an experience of losing one's way in the woods in the middle of life's journey. Some Arthurian legends portray a middle-aged Arthur stranded in the midst of a forest. Frequently people reach their middle years having accomplished the goals they had set as young adults, but now feel uncertain about what new objectives to set. Others find that goals they once imagined would provide a sense of satisfaction now seem hollow or empty. They feel "at a loss" to know what goals—or values—to put in their place. Some encounter unforeseen circumstances—the loss of a job, a relationship, or their health—that leave them feeling disoriented. They have been robbed of the landmarks they had relied on. Still others find that their lives have taken on the dullness of routine. The well-worn path has lost its appeal, and the prospect of straying from it to enjoy an adventure in unknown territory is tantalizing.

A third life stage that can induce a feeling of being lost is old age. This stage of life can bring many kinds of "diminishment": moving from larger (and more familiar) accommodations to smaller ones; increasing dependency on family members; losses of hearing, mobility, independence, and mental acuity. These losses can produce a feeling of lostness and insecurity. If "the path" represents the things that are familiar, many people as they age will feel the loss of the signposts and landmarks that have helped them to get their bearings.

In addition to the experiences of lostness that are typical of particular periods of life, any one of us can be "thrown for a loop" by some unexpected calamity. A serious accident or illness that befalls you or someone close to you, the takeover of the company you work for, an assault or a break-in at your home or workplace—any of these events can challenge your assumptions about what can be relied on in life. A common response to a serious loss in life is grief, and a common characteristic of grief is a feeling of confusion or disorientation, a feeling of being lost.

Finding Yourself Lost

These experiences of feeling lost are primarily not of our choosing. In Chapter 2 we encountered Franklin, the storybook turtle whose parents warned him not to go into the woods alone. When he played a game of hide and seek with his friends, Franklin became distracted and "without even thinking...walked right into the woods." It might be more accurately said that he was thinking of something else, or that his mind was elsewhere. Franklin looked up and suddenly realized that he didn't know where he was or how he got there. The familiar landmarks were gone. "Every tree looked the same. Every rock looked the same. He couldn't find the path." When, after a good deal of searching, his parents found him, they reminded him that they had warned him not to go into the woods alone. "'It wasn't on purpose,' sniffled Franklin. 'I was looking for Fox and I forgot.'"[1]

Often when one gets lost in life it is not "on purpose." There is no intent to stray from the path, but perhaps something distracts you. Or you can't see the forest for the trees. You become preoccupied with the day-to-day without realizing that a pattern is forming that leads inexorably away from the path you thought you were on. Or circumstances beyond your control leave you feeling that you have lost your bearings or have entered unfamiliar territory. Suddenly—or gradually—you wake up to that "I'm not in Kansas anymore" feeling.

How can that sense of lostness that may come unbidden and against your will be addressed? When the cause of your disorientation is clear to you and to the people who know you—bereavement, the loss of a job, or the end of a relationship—friends and loved ones may rally around. They may reach out and remind you of familiar things that can help you to get on track again. If you feel like a victim of change, they can help you to remember what has not changed.

But when your inner feelings of being lost—or their sources—are harder to define, the people around you may be less aware of your need for reassurance and a renewed sense of direction. You may need help articulating what you feel and what your soul requires. It may help to get reoriented by revisiting familiar places or by reconnecting with people who have known you for a long time. You might seek out the help of a professional who can be a guide as you work through a sense of dis-ease.

There may be no shortcuts back to the path that you have lost. In fact, finding your way again may involve discovering a new path altogether. In any case, a sense of dislocation may have to be given time to be worked out. It may be a needful episode that keeps you from getting stuck in a rut, helps you to discover a more authentic way of living, or moves you forward in your life. A sense of being lost is not a pleasant feeling, but in order to grow as a person, you may need to resist the impulse to end the pain by seeking a quick fix.

It can take time to move from a sense of being lost to a sense of being found, or from having lost something to having found something. But however long it takes, that is usually the progression we are inclined to follow. Being lost feels like a dilemma; being found, like the solution. We seek a resolution of a situation that does not feel right. With guidance from friends and professionals, from our inner resources, or from a sense that God's Spirit is present to guide us, the outcome we seek is one in which the lost is found.

The Christian scriptures portray God as an active player searching for the lost. Luke's gospel tells a series of stories of things that have been lost and of a figure (who represents God) looking for them. A shepherd goes in search of a lost sheep (Luke 15:3–7). A woman turns her house upside down looking for a lost coin (Luke 15:8–10). And a father awaits a lost, prodigal son and runs to meet him when he sees the young man finally coming home (Luke 15:11–32).

These stories portray God as an active seeker of those who have lost their way. In each story, the desired outcome is that what is lost should be found, and there is rejoicing when the outcome is achieved.

But one difference among the stories is the degree to which each of the lost "items" bears responsibility for getting lost in the first place. As an inanimate object, the coin has made no decisions in regard to its fate. Clearly it did not get lost "on purpose"; nor did it contribute to being found. The sheep has a degree of consciousness, but perhaps not enough intelligence to realize the dangers that could result from wandering off. But the prodigal son has made the most deliberate choice. He has set his own "lostness" in motion by taking his share of his father's estate and going to a far country. And he is the one who makes the crucial decision to return home to seek his father's forgiveness.

Straying on Purpose

The last of these three stories is a reminder that getting lost in life is sometimes a consequence of choices one has made. It is "on purpose." Whether as rebellious adolescents or as middle-aged people bored with life, many of us have wandered off and gone deliberately astray. Some may have sought adventure or dismissed the prevailing values of their family or their society. Some have decided that they needed to discover what is important for themselves rather than accepting the maxims passed on by their elders. Some have rejected the path that others have laid out for them and insisted on the right to make their own choices and their own way.

People's reasons for "wandering" may seem perfectly valid to them. But to others, it may look like they have gone off the rails, that they need to come to their senses and return to more conventional patterns of behaviour. In an Italian folk tale called "Solomon's Advice," the sage Solomon gives a storekeeper a series of apparently irrelevant pieces of advice, each of which turns out to be useful in an unexpected way. The first of these—"Don't leave the old road for a new one"—leads the storekeeper to decline an invitation to join some new friends on their travels. The travellers end up being murdered by brigands. Psychiatrist Allan B. Chinen, in *Once Upon a Midlife*, reads Solomon's advice as a warning against too frequent experimentation, whether with romances or with jobs.

To be sure, sometimes straying is merely something to be gotten out of one's system and is followed by a return to a more conventional way of living. But for some people, straying from the path may lead to new territory from which they never return. Those from whom they become estranged in this process regard them as lost, but they themselves are quite content where they are.

In both history and fiction, forests are home to hunters, woodcutters, and hermits—people who had been marginalized by society, but who generally lived in the woods by choice. Others may have regarded them as strange people living in a strange place, but they were largely content to live where they did. Similarly, Europeans and North Americans in David Livingstone's time had a sense that he had gotten himself lost somewhere in the jungles of Africa. But all the time Dr. Livingstone knew exactly where he was and had chosen to be there.

Sometimes going intentionally astray reflects different lifestyle choices or an intention to be true to ourselves and our values. We are not really lost and do not need to be found. At other times, though, people may feel lost as a consequence of reckless or purely selfish decisions, and can understand their experience—at the time or in retrospect—as a case of having lost their moral compass.

Such actions may be a response to disillusionment. An experience may have left a feeling that nothing matters very much. Whatever the cause, you may live your life for a period in a kind of moral chaos, in ways that suggest no sense of responsibility or accountability to other people. Sometimes being found depends on returning to a sense of who you really are and what you are really worth. The story of the prodigal son puts this beautifully when, suddenly recognizing where straying has led him, the young man "came to himself" (Luke 15:17). In literature this is called a moment of tragic illumination, a moment in which reality sets in. And it may be a necessary moment if one who is lost is to be found.

Some people, though, may live a "lost life" for some time without realizing it or being very much concerned about it. The chorus from Handel's *Messiah*, "All We Like Sheep Have Gone Astray," draws its text from the Book of Isaiah (53:6). In setting it to music, Handel composed a sprightly tune that conveys the wanderings of thoughtless creatures who "have turned every one to his own way." The story is told that when the eccentric English conductor Sir Thomas Beecham took a choir through this chorus in rehearsal, the singers captured the irresponsibility of the sheep almost *too* well. "When we sing 'All we like sheep have gone astray,'" he said, "might we please have a little more regret and a little less satisfaction?"

To be fair to Handel, the cheerful chorus comes to a dead stop and the tempo changes to a solemn adagio at the words "and the Lord hath laid on Him the iniquity of us all." It is as if the people who are "like sheep" have that sudden moment of tragic illumination. They finally see the consequences of their actions and come to themselves. They identify their situation as one of being lost and are ready to be found.

The stories in Luke suggest that, in the meantime, someone has been out looking for them. Certainly it is usual, when someone goes missing in the bush, for a search party to be organized. And when people we care about appear to become lost in their lives—whether accidentally or by design—we may attempt to intervene. We may search for them or at least hope they will return.

Whether it is a child momentarily lost track of in a supermarket or a loved one lost for years to substance abuse or another form of self-destructive behaviour, it is not only the one who is lost who can feel anxiety, frustration, anger, and guilt. Those who search actively or who merely wait helplessly can feel these things, too. And if there is rejoicing when the story ends happily and the lost is found, there can be sorrow if the story ends badly. Or there can be a roller coaster of emotions when it feels like the story will go on forever, with no resolution in sight.

When the Path Leaves You

In the second act of the musical *Into the Woods*, the fairy-tale characters find themselves contending with a dangerous, destructive giant. One of them, Little Red Ridinghood, regrets the decision that got her into this situation and turned her world upside down. Her mother had warned her not to stray from the path, she reflects. But the Baker corrects her. It is the path that has strayed from her, he says.

Sometimes people feel that the world—or some significant aspect of it—is rolling along without them and has left them behind. They can experience the same feelings of lostness—alienation, loneliness, abandonment—as when they or someone they care about has wandered from the path.

When Britain introduced decimalized currency in the early 1970s, an old woman committed suicide. Feeling increasingly marginalized by changes that were taking place in the world she lived in, she left a note that said decimalization was the last straw. When a man I know retired a few years ago, he said that he had achieved his ambition of retiring without becoming computer literate. The world was moving in a direction that was strange and unfamiliar to him, and he elected not to go with it.

It isn't just changes in the way the world works, advances in technology, or "progress" that can leave you feeling sidelined. Over the years, you may come to feel more and more out of step with the prevailing attitudes or values of society. Or you may work hard for an organization for years only to see the leadership take it in a new direction that departs from its original vision. It feels as if the path has strayed from you. The decisions that others have made can leave you feeling angry, displaced, or simply sad. I can think of three retired men who have spoken to me about this kind of experience.

An older man in a congregation I once served was disturbed by many changes that had been taking place in the denomination in recent years. He felt bewildered and disoriented by it all and unable to influence decisions and events. "I'm not going to leave the church," he said to me sadly. "But sometimes I feel like the church has left me."

Another retired man revealed his feeling of near-despair that the kind of Christianity he had tried to promote over the years was being swamped by the "religious right" in North America. He felt overwhelmed by the power of this element in the society of his time, and by how little room was left for the kind of spiritual values that were important to him.

Still another retired man lamented that his contemporaries saw their retirement as an opportunity to leave behind concern about the world and the needs of other people. Their retirement plans focused on comfortable surroundings and an abundance of travel and leisure activities. But there was no time for volunteering or advocating on behalf of the weaker members of society. They might have been concerned about social issues at other stages in their lives, but now their circles of concern had shrunk. They had isolated themselves from the world and its needs. The man who described this situation to me felt isolated, too. In continuing to work at the things he still believed were important, he felt that he had been abandoned by the people who had once shared his passion. The path the others were on had left him.

Perhaps the experiences of these three men resonate with you. So may their feelings of isolation and lostness. Whether they responded by withdrawing from life or carried on in support of the things that mattered to them, they found life to be challenging in ways they had not expected. They had to look into their souls and decide whether to face the future with resignation or with hope.

For personal reflection or group discussion

1. Have you ever felt that you had lost your way in life? Identify some of the factors that contributed to that feeling.

2. Have you ever been concerned about someone who is close to you who seemed to have wandered from the path? What have you desired for them? How have you expressed that desire?

3. Can you relate to the feeling that it is the path that has strayed from you? Have you ever felt left out or left behind by the world or by your circle of friends? How have you dealt with that feeling?

chapter 5

a clearing in the forest
discernment in times of transition

On a beautiful summer's day, a group of us made our way up the switch-backs of a winding mountain trail west of Banff, Alberta. Again and again the path turned back on itself as it wound through the trees. We could see only a very short distance in any direction through the densely wooded forest. The sensation was one of being enclosed, of literally being unable to see the forest for the trees. Although the woods were pleasantly cool, after a couple of hours of climbing I began to feel somewhat oppressed. But finally, I felt a welcome sense of relief as the path emerged into a broad, expansive alpine meadow. As we stepped out of the trees into this clear space, we were able not only to look back at the woods through which we had come, but to see the forest retreating on all sides of us. Our perspective changed. We felt able to pause and catch our breath, to rest and consider our next steps.

"A CLEARING IN THE FOREST" is the title of a reflective paper Derek Evans wrote after making the transition from Deputy Secretary General of Amnesty International, based in London, England, to director of The United Church of Canada's Naramata Centre in the Okanagan Valley of British Columbia. Subtitled "An Experience of Discernment in a Time of Personal Transition," the paper uses a telling incident in Derek's working life as its point of departure.[1]

On a mission to Guatemala, Derek and a colleague met with the father of one of the "disappeared," a university student who had been taken from his classroom in broad daylight by the police and had not been seen since. Derek did everything that his 20 years with Amnesty International had taught him to do: check facts, prepare documents, and so on. After meeting for an hour with the father, a silence fell on the three of them. The father looked down at his hands and began to weep. Derek and his colleague exchanged a silent glance and, both of them parents, got up and quietly embraced the man. They knew that, in the face of such grief, any words would sound trite.

Derek knew at the time that he felt emotionally exhausted and even a little resentful of the demands of the situation. Later, a colleague commented that he had seemed a bit reserved, perhaps withholding part of himself. Later still, he was able to look back on this experience as a "triggering incident" that marked the beginning of a transition in his life.

There really are times when you can't see the forest for the trees. The day-to-day patterns of living are so close that you fail to ask basic questions or seek a larger perspective. But sooner or later you may realize that the patterns you have known—however familiar, pleasant, or useful they have been—are not working anymore. You may come to such a point in your career, in a relationship, or in where you wish to live at a particular stage. At times like that, you need not to leave the forest, perhaps, but to find a space within it—a clearing—in order to discern where to go next. A clearing is not always a comfortable place to be. The Hebrew scriptures describe the action of clearing a forest as a tactic that leaves people with nowhere to hide. And that may be how you feel in life's transitional phases.

Sometimes, like Derek Evans, you can identify a triggering incident that marks the beginning of a transition. That incident may be evident at the time it happens, or sensed only in retrospect. The incident may have an external source—it happens to you. You lose a job. An accident or illness reduces your capacity to live independently. A spouse dies or decides to end the relationship. You are propelled into a period of transition against your will by an event that you did not choose.

Other times of transition have an internal source. They may be linked in your mind to a particular event, which will take on meaning in your personal mythology. You have a dawning realization that your inner feelings and attitudes are changing. You experience a growing sense of dissatisfaction or feelings of depression or malaise. Or you simply sense that a chapter of your life is ending, that a particular phase has run its course.

It may take a while to see that you have entered a time when changes need to be made and there are decisions to make. Like Derek, you may have a significant degree of "say" in the decisions about where to go next. You may even have the luxury of time. With no one rushing you, you can consider your options carefully and look and listen for sources of guidance as you step from the wooded path to spend time in the clearing.

Creating Space

Where can you find those sources of guidance? How can you create space for discernment? When you have a sense that something needs to change but do not yet know what the change should be, you can become restless and frustrated. But the "meantime"—the time that must elapse before the way ahead becomes clear—can be used profitably rather than merely endured.

A great resource in a time of transition can be an ability to live in the present. Some people find it difficult to be patient during the discomfort that a transitional period can bring. You may long for the future in which this uncomfortable period will be over. In imagination you may project yourself forward weeks or years to a time when these uncertainties will be resolved. In this fantasy world, everything will be better. Or alternatively, you may fall prey to fears and anxieties, imagining the worst, feeling that the situation will only deteriorate.

Caught between your hopes and fears for the future, you may need to remind yourself that the present is the only time you are really given. It is only by making the most of the present time that you can influence the future that holds either unreasonable hopes or unreasonable fears.

When my children were small, my sister-in-law took a photograph of them sitting in front of the fireplace in their grandparents' home. She placed the picture in a folder on which she wrote the words "Yesterday is ashes, tomorrow is wood; only today the flame burns brightly." The present is all we have, and our use of the present can alter the future. In fact, even when a breakthrough is slow in coming, there are things that can be done here and now that will move you toward it, however imperceptible your progress may seem at times.

In order to step back from the trees, sometimes you need to do something solitary. In biblical terms, spending time alone in a wilderness is an experience that presents challenges, but it also provides an opportunity for introspection and sorting out priorities. When Jesus was led into the wilderness by the Spirit, this was to be a good and necessary experience for him. The accounts of this experience in Matthew and Luke describe Jesus sorting out his priorities as he answers the devil's suggestions about using his talents and conducting his life's work. In his responses, Jesus rejects the devil's appeal to short-sighted self-interest.

A clearing, like the biblical wilderness, is a place for deep reflection and for getting in touch with inner resources. In transition times, you need to find time for yourself. Some people find it helpful to put some distance, literally, between themselves and the regular routine of their lives. Jesus, for example, was led to a space that was geographically removed from the area where he lived and worked in order to focus on a particular spiritual task. Getting away for a change of scene, going on a retreat, or returning to a place that has had spiritual significance in the past are things that can help. But even a small time-out, like going for a long walk, can provide an opportunity for reflection. And if, when you feel unproductive, you can find some activity that uses a part of your brain or your body that you do not use much of the time, you may discover an added bonus. Derek Evans found working in his garden produced something at a time when he felt unproductive. More than that, clearing out the undergrowth, digging up choking weeds, and letting the sun shine on darkened corners acted out a metaphor for his life.

The gift of "meantime" that a clearing provides can be a reminder of the importance of exercise and care for our bodies. If you feel a sense of depression or ennui in a transition time, it is very easy to become a couch potato and pay little attention to what your body needs. Taking time to walk, swim, or go to a gym are ways of strengthening your inner resources so that the meantime can be used well.

Companions in the Clearing

If the clearing in the forest is a place to spend some time in solitude, it may also be a place where you need company on occasion. A woman I know entered a stress leave from work feeling depressed and uncertain whether she would return to her job or look for something new. It would have been easy for her to give in to anti-social feelings and shun the company of others. But during her leave she maintained her pattern of attending weekly choir practice. She used her voice and expressed her feelings through music with a group of people whom she regarded as her "chosen family." This activity helped her to maintain her equilibrium as she tried to discern the way ahead. In fact, she described the musical companionship she found in her choir involvement as a "lifesaver."

In transitional times, we need to make space for companions, fellow travellers, people we can talk to and bounce some ideas around with. Professional counsellors or therapists can help us make sense of the trees when we feel overwhelmed by the forest, or to see the pattern of the forest when all we can see are individual trees with no relation to one another. Those of us who have engaged in a counselling process know that sometimes we can feel stuck for a long period, questioning whether we will ever be able to move forward. But, as we often realize later, things were percolating even when we were unaware of it.

Psychologists suggest that, while our conscious minds may gather information, it is our unconscious minds that integrate that information and lead us to better and more satisfying decisions. And our unconscious minds need time to work with this information before they can produce results. What may seem to be a sudden and spontaneous breakthrough is in fact the result of unseen processes finally coming to their moment of fruition.

In common speech, the biblical terms "epiphany" and "a Damascus-road experience" are used to suggest a sudden and spontaneous breakthrough. But the original Epiphany, the moment of arrival when the magi came to see the baby Jesus, was the culmination of a long, difficult, and necessary journey. And the life-changing encounter with the Spirit of Christ on the road to Damascus (Acts 9) of Saul of Tarsus, later known as the apostle Paul, came only after a long period in which he had denied Jesus' claims on his life by persecuting followers of "the way."

As we wait for breakthroughs and moments of insight to come, not only may we be helped by professionals, we can also benefit from conversations with family and friends. Not everyone will offer the same kind of advice, and some will speak out of their own agendas. This is where it is important to be able to discern which voice speaks the message that really needs to be heard. Derek Evans' colleagues all thought he should stay with Amnesty. The only person who sensed that he needed to move on was his wife, the person who knew him best.

There was a similar experience in my parents' lives. After working for over 20 years as a minister, my father was invited to join the editorial staff of a newspaper. The opportunity appealed to his interests as a writer. However, after thinking long and hard about it, he decided to decline the invitation and wrote the publisher to inform him. My father gave the letter to my mother to mail. The next day, he told her that he was feeling that he had made the wrong decision and wished he could reconsider. After their many years of marriage, my mother knew my father well enough to sense that he had not been entirely comfortable with his decision of the previous day. When he voiced his second thoughts, she was able to give him back the letter that she had been carrying in her purse. She had decided not to mail it until he had time for those second thoughts.

It is good to have people in your life who know you, in a sense, better than you know yourself. It is good to have people to talk to, but it is better still to know whose opinions to trust. The people whose opinions matter—or *should* matter—may not all be part of your current circle of family and friendship. As he sought clarity in his situation, Derek Evans called to mind the most influential teachers of his formative years, the ones who had inspired him, perceived his gifts, and encouraged their development. Although he had not had contact with these teachers for many years, he decided, as an exercise, to write them a letter to report on the course his life had taken. He wrote it in a way that would make sense to people who had known him but who had had no hand in recent events in his life. The exercise revealed links between his present life and work and some of the core values and ideals of his youth. For him the value in the exercise was not in actually sending the letter (although he did send it), but in the clarity (the "clearing") and the sense of direction that it provided.

Derek's letter-writing exercise helped access a sense of discernment that came from reviewing his life and putting his present transitional stage in context. Sometimes things can become clearer in your life if you can take time to look backwards as well as forwards. The path that brought you to this clearing may provide guidance as you seek the path that will take you out of it. Looking back, you may discern a thread running through your life. Gifts and abilities, values and influences, and beliefs and convictions have helped shape your life to this point. If these things are still valid for you, you may be able to extrapolate from this point into the future. What is past may be a prologue to the next phase of your life. And if some of the things you thought were important no longer are, you may sense yourself being called to a more authentic life. Your new priorities and choices will better reflect the person you now feel called to be.

Proceeding with Caution

It is important when facing a transition in life to know what to do and where to look for direction. But it is also important to know what not to do. Derek Evans learned not to be rash. The best decisions are rarely made as an impulsive reaction to a bad situation.

Perhaps in a time of transition you have been energized by the ending of some responsibilities and the freedom of entertaining new possibilities. At times like that, people may explore opportunities to fulfill some dream that they had long ago set aside. But this is where it becomes important to test the dreams carefully. Opening a bed and breakfast, turning your carpentry hobby into a career, reconnecting with an old boyfriend or girlfriend who has never entirely left your dreams: these may all be appealing ideas. But do your research to see how practical the dream may be. Some things might satisfy you as an avocation, but would no longer be fulfilling as a full-time occupation. It is good to distinguish between romance and reality.

There is wisdom as well in not settling for a superficial change. Sometimes people move from one job to another, from one home to another, or from one partner to another without addressing the inner issues. This just takes the old problems along into a new situation. When the novelty of the new situation has worn off, nothing has really changed.

I once met a man in his forties who was married to his fourth wife. Someone who knew him better than I did said, "John hasn't had four marriages. He's just had the same marriage four times, because he never learns anything." Transition times are opportunities to look within and not just to rearrange the furniture. They are times for careful reflection rather than knee-jerk reactions or band-aid solutions.

As someone who went through the ending of a marriage myself, I believe that the significant period of time that elapsed between the day my wife and I first raised the possibility of separating and the actual separation enabled us both to devote time to learning about ourselves. As a result, even such a difficult and painful transition took on some redemptive qualities.

Finding a clearing in the forest in transition times can address an essential human need: the need to feel that your life is significant, that you make a difference. The things that are part of the "journey inward"—that deepen your understanding of your inner person—can add to a sense of the significance your life has to yourself. And the things that you do as part of your "journey outward"—the things that make a positive difference to the people around you—can add to your sense of the significance your life has to the world.

Small wonder that people who enter a transition time in their lives often sense that they are looking for a way to have a greater and more positive impact on other people. It is perhaps a search for a way to leave a legacy that matters.

The Quiet Centre

In recent years, there has been a reawakening of interest, among Christians and others, in one particular type of "clearing." Many people have found the solitary spiritual practice of walking a labyrinth to be an aid to discernment. A labyrinth is a circular path that doubles back on itself again and again until the walker arrives at the centre. Many modern labyrinths are modelled on the one at Chartres Cathedral in France. For example, a well-known copy of the Chartres labyrinth is in Grace Episcopal Cathedral in San Francisco. In North America, labyrinths are often indoors, in sanctuaries or church halls. Others are outdoors, laid out on a lawn, in a garden, or even on a plaza in a city centre.

Whatever the setting or the material used to create the labyrinth, many people have benefited from walking the path, praying, meditating, or simply clearing their minds as they walk. Some approach their walk with a particular question in mind, a question that relates to their need for discernment. When they reach the centre, they might pause for some time before retracing their steps. The centre can be like a clearing in a forest, a still point where you can stop, look, and listen. Here you can be still and become aware of the resources within you and around you until the way to go becomes clear.

For personal reflection or group discussion

1. At times when you have needed to discern the way ahead, where have you turned for guidance? How did you know which voices to trust?

2. Can you think of practices that have helped you create a "clearing in the forest" when you have gone through a time of transition? What insights have you gained about yourself through these practices?

3. If someone who was going through a life transition asked you for advice, can you think of anything from your experience or observation that you would advise them *not* to do?

chapter 6

lions and tigers, and big bad wolves
the faces of fear

My daughter, Katie, recounts this experience from her high school days: My mother and I were walking through the ravine near our house one evening when we heard a strange howling sound. We convinced ourselves it was just some kids having a party nearby. As we walked on, it became increasingly evident that we were hearing not the sound of rowdy teens but the doleful howls of a pack of coyotes. We soon found ourselves sprinting all the way out of the woods.

A CLOSE ENCOUNTER with a pack of coyotes is a fearful though unexceptional experience for people who live in Alberta, where this incident took place. Less common in that part of the world but more deadly are attacks by grizzlies and cougars. But the forests of imagination are inhabited by an even wider variety of scary creatures. In the movie version of *The Wizard of Oz*, when the Yellow Brick Road leads Dorothy and her friends through a forest, they begin to tremble at the thought of "lions and tigers and bears." In European folk tales, the animal most often used to inspire fear in the heart of a child is the wolf. From "Little Red Ridinghood" to "The Three Little Pigs" to "Peter and the Wolf," the wolf has been presented—fairly or not—as the bogey that plays on childhood fears.

Forest Fears

In previous chapters, the woods were described as a forbidden place—because we may get lost in the forest or lose our innocence there. But the woods may also be a forbidden place because of other dangers lurking among the trees. For Dante, the forest itself was frightening. An earlier description of the forest as a negative agent is recounted in the Hebrew scriptures. When the army of King David's son, Absalom, took on his father's forces in the thickets and difficult terrain of the forest of Ephraim, "the forest claimed more victims that day than the sword" (2 Samuel 18:8).

Whatever you make of that enigmatic assertion, it is clear that in biblical times it was common for an enemy to hide in a forest. For that reason, to eliminate the threat of such an enemy the forest would sometimes be cleared so that it could no longer provide cover or refuge. Joshua, for example, in speaking to some of the tribes of Israel, promises that "the hill country shall be yours, for though it is a forest, you shall clear it and possess it to its farthest border; for you shall drive out the Canaanites" (Joshua 17:18).

Forests can also be a haven for wild animals that fill us with dread. Ezekiel is one biblical writer who foresees a time when God will deal with this threat. He imagines God declaring of his flock, "I will make with them a covenant of peace and banish wild animals from the land, so that they may live in the wild and sleep in the woods securely" (Ezekiel 34:25).

Elsewhere, though, scripture portrays God siding with the wild animals against the humans. When several boys dare to mock the prophet Elisha, no sooner does God's messenger curse them than two she-bears come out of the woods and maul them (2 Kings 2:23–24). The horror of episodes like these is increased by the suggestion that, far from protecting us from such attacks, God uses wild animals as instruments of judgment against sinful people. Railing on God's behalf against the disobedience of the people of Jerusalem, for example, Jeremiah declares with some satisfaction, "therefore a lion from the forest shall kill them" (Jeremiah 5:6).

In Jesus' wilderness story, he is described as having to contend "with the wild beasts" (Mark 1:13). The beasts may be understood as his adversaries, just as angels are presented as his allies. And he has a more major adversary: the devil. Similarly, in folklore the forest creatures that can threaten our well-being are not limited to wild beasts. There are monsters as well, trolls and other semi-human or supernatural creatures. Centuries ago Christian imagination took the god Pan—a woodland spirit in the form of a goat complete with horns, beard, and cloven feet—and found in him a pictorial representation of the devil. This pagan god, this half-man and half-beast who invented the shepherd's pipe and sported on the mountains, could also inspire a rush of fear (pan-ic) by his sudden appearance. But when his features were appropriated for depictions of the devil, the horned one lost any semblance of playfulness and was reduced to a source of menace.

Whether as a refuge for human adversaries, the habitat of wild animals, or the imagined locus of malevolent beings, one thing forests have come to symbolize over the centuries is what we fear. We all have fears in our lives; it is not surprising that woodland stories telling of frightening encounters—from the Gilgamesh epic onwards—are so universally compelling.

The Things We Fear

The childhood fears addressed in so many fairy tales point to fears that are carried into adulthood. In stories set in a forest, the protagonist may experience abandonment ("Hansel and Gretel") or conflict and violence ("Little Red Ridinghood"). A character who faces a loss of control or destruction by superior forces can evoke a more general fear of the loss of the familiar. The forest, as a mysterious place, often plays upon a fear of the unknown. In the forest, order gives way to chaos. Unlike a town or a city where human beings can decide the nature of things, fictional forests are places where the outcomes cannot be controlled. They can be chaotic places where things no longer make sense. When urban settings produce violent or disordered situations, forest imagery is used to describe this unwelcome reality. "It's a jungle out there," we say.

The fears of adults tend to focus on the things that cannot be controlled or predicted. Life as you know it changes, in a way that you did not effect yourself. Think of the things you fear most in life. A major illness or incapacity, serious harm befalling a beloved child, the death of someone you depend on: any of these may take you by surprise. And each of them threatens diminishment to one degree or another. A fear of failure, of rejection or humiliation, of being "found out" or of losing face: these are variations on the fear of diminishment in the eyes of others—and in your own eyes as well. Fear of commitment to a relationship, a job, or a cause is a fear that your capacity to make independent decisions about the direction of your life will be compromised.

Putting Fears in Their Place

Maurice Sendak's popular children's story *Where the Wild Things Are* describes a little boy named Max. One night, having behaved wildly while wearing his wolf suit, Max is sent to bed without his supper. In a dreamlike sequence, his bedroom is transformed into a forest and Max is transported to the place where the wild things are. These monsters seem frightening at first, but Max gains mastery over them. He tells them to be still and subdues them by staring into their eyes without blinking. He tells them when to start their wild rumpus and when to stop it. They declare him king of the wild things and are saddened when he has to leave.

Max puts his fears in their place by staring them down. It is important for all of us to put our fears in their place. The difficulty is that not all fears belong in the same place, and it requires discernment to figure out what to do with any particular fear. A phobia—an irrational fear like claustrophobia, for instance—may be dealt with by means of extensive psychotherapy or by simply avoiding enclosed spaces. Which is better? It may depend on just how incapacitating the fear is.

Some of our fears themselves diminish our lives, and often unnecessarily. That may be one meaning of Franklin Delano Roosevelt's famous aphorism that all we have to fear is fear itself. People may not suffer from a phobia in a clinical sense, but nonetheless allow vain imaginings to rule them and limit their options.

We may exaggerate the power of certain things to threaten us. It has often been suggested that the wolves who are cast as the "heavies" in so many children's stories have been given a bad rap. When a wolf was suspected of killing a young man in the woods of northern Saskatchewan in November 2005, it was pointed out that, if a wolf had indeed been the culprit, it would have been the first time a human had been killed by a wolf in North America in over 100 years.

Kenneth Grahame's classic story *The Wind in the Willows* includes a map by illustrator Ernest Shepherd on which the area known as the Wild Wood is labelled "Weasels and Stoats." To be sure, these woodland animals could pose a threat to the riverbank creatures. But when, in the chapter entitled "The Wild Wood," Mole disregards the Water Rat's advice and strays into the wood, it is not these animals but his imagination that causes his fears to run away with him. Stumps take on the appearance of caricatures; holes look like ugly mouths. He discovers what Rat had tried to shield him from: the terror of the Wild Wood.

For Mole much of the terror was a creation of his anxious mind. And many people know what it is to allow a fear to become bigger than it deserves to be. You may have found that naming the fear and talking it out with someone has cut it down to size. Perhaps one of our reasons for being put here on this earth—along with bearing one another's burdens—is to lighten one another's fears. You may have discovered that, when the thing you dreaded finally came to pass, it was not as powerful as you had imagined it to be. Somewhere along the way, you must have found the resources to meet it when it came.

In the novel *To Kill a Mockingbird*, Harper Lee recounts a story of misplaced fear. Atticus Finch, a widowed, small town lawyer in the deep south during the Great Depression, is asked to defend a Black man, falsely accused of rape. Bob Ewell, the father of the man's accuser, takes a bitter dislike to Atticus for defending the man. Meanwhile, Atticus's two children, a boy named Jem and a girl nicknamed Scout, are fascinated by a mysterious neighbour—a strange, reclusive young man known as "Boo" Radley. Although the children have never seen him, they have heard scary stories about his behaviour. One night, walking home through the woods, the children are attacked by one man and rescued by another. Their attacker is a man about whom they know little—Bob Ewell—but the identity of their rescuer comes as a surprise. It is the young man whom they had taught themselves to fear: Boo Radley. One whom they imagined wished them harm turns out to have wished them good.

You, too, may have had occasion to learn that someone you feared—someone who seemed "different," perhaps—was not as frightening as you had imagined. You may have discovered that your fears were unfounded or misplaced. Such discoveries should teach us, among other things, to be wary of attempts made by others to inspire fear. For example, why would adherents of one religion want to encourage fear of the adherents of another? What might a government have to gain by fostering in its people a fear of terrorism or of a different political system?

Sometimes lions and tigers do not warrant the fear they inspire. When Dorothy, the Scarecrow, and the Tin Woodman were considering the possibility that such creatures might inhabit the woods, they were indeed beset by a lion. But it turned out to be a cowardly one whose bluff was called soon enough. A tiger sometimes turns out to be just a paper tiger after all.

Not that all fear is false or unwarranted. In fact, fear of the right things is healthy. Life brings its share of genuine "dangers, toils, and snares" (as the hymn "Amazing Grace" describes them), and we do well to pay attention to the danger signs and proceed with caution. The "fight or flight" response to a threat may be hard-wired into our psyches for a purpose. To cite that old hymn again, it is grace that teaches our hearts to fear. A fear of the right things may be a way that God provides for our well-being. Putting fear in its place means identifying those things that do warrant being afraid, and acting accordingly.

Where Fear Can Lead

Only by facing the things that deserve to inspire fear can you push past the fear to some new place. When a fear is occasioned by a change that is not within your control, it is well to keep in mind the saying that although change is inevitable, growth is an option. Many of the things you fear, though they may merit it, provide an opportunity for growth. They can lead you to some new and better place in your life if you are willing to be led there.

In the Disney film of *Beauty and the Beast*, Belle's father sets out with his horse to sell one of his inventions. His route takes him through the woods. Beginning to lose his way, he comes to a signpost with several signs pointing in different directions, but the writing on all of them has been rubbed out. He looks down each of two paths. One is dark and eerie; the other is better lit and less spooky. His horse tries to go down the easier road, but Belle's father leads him down the more frightening one. Before long they are attacked by bats, chased by wolves, and almost fall off a cliff. The horse runs away, and the wolves chase the inventor to the beast's castle. And so Belle's father moves through his terrors and fears and arrives at the right place—the place he is meant to be—after all.

My daughter, Katie—who provided the vignette that opened this chapter—spent the year following high school working with an organization called Katimavik. With a group of other young people, she volunteered in a series of three different communities across the country. In the first two towns she worked with children and enjoyed it. But in her last assignment she was asked to work in a care home. The prospect of attending to the needs of the elderly and the infirm was less welcome. In fact she felt intimidated and unequal to the task. But contrary to her expectations, before long she found herself enjoying the work and the people. Soon after entering university the next year, she was talking about going into social work and specializing in gerontology. A challenge that had been unwelcome—and even frightening—ended up leading her into a new place in her life.

The Judeo-Christian scriptures are full of incidents in which people move through fear to something better—a destination that they had not foreseen. The Bible recounts many stories of people experiencing something that alarms them and responding initially with fear. Often the alarm is caused by the appearance of an angel bringing some announcement. The people receiving this visitation typically greet it with fear; the angel invariably has to tell them not to be afraid. For example, this is the sequence when the angel Gabriel appears to Mary to tell her that she is to give birth to Jesus, and in Matthew's account of an angel appearing to the women who visit Jesus' tomb after the crucifixion.

This pattern suggests that it is not just bad changes that scare us; good ones can frighten us as well. Both of these incidents announce a changed situation—one that those who are visited cannot control, but that will demand something of them all the same. Perhaps both Mary and the people who came to the tomb would just as soon have been left alone. Their lives would have been less exciting and certainly less hopeful, but they would have had the comfort of the familiar. But both stories are about the promise of new life. Once the participants get past the shock of a changed situation, their fear gives way to joy and to active participation in a new reality. Those of us who fear commitment to a person or a thing may be able to relate to the fear they felt. But we may also learn something from the fact that it was their commitment to a new reality that led them to a new life.

It is not uncommon for people who are diagnosed with a life-threatening illness to experience fear. However, those same people can often push through to another level, or shift into a higher gear, in which life is lived with a greater sense of purpose and intensity. Life takes on a different quality when you sense that you have nothing left to lose.

Gay men and lesbians who have "come out" often record a similar feeling. After living closeted lives for years, fearful of the consequences of exposure, we have found that finally taking the leap and being honest about ourselves has been exhilarating. Not only has the world not come crashing down; we have discovered a freedom and an authenticity in our lives that we had not known before.

Often, confronting the thing that was feared gives life a focus. When troubling physical symptoms are diagnosed, you know at last what you are dealing with and can channel your energies into dealing with it. When you take the plunge and reveal something secret about yourself, you are no longer left wondering whether people's benign attitudes toward you are based on a false understanding of who you really are. When you commit yourself to a relationship, a cause, or a way of life that is bigger than yourself, you discover that all you have lost is a sense of meaninglessness. Rather than the diminishment you feared, your life takes on an added significance.

The Call of the Wild

The old gospel hymn "Just As I Am" speaks of "fightings and fears within, without." Most of the fears discussed in this chapter have been of things "without"—both beyond our control and beyond our selves. But another kind of fear is a fear of something within. Forces that are wild, uncontrollable, and possibly destructive are not always external. In *Where the Wild Things Are*, not only is there wildness in the monsters who live far away; there is wildness in the little boy in the wolf suit. There is wildness in Max himself.

Wild animals inhabit the forests of imagination, but there is also "the beast within." Fictional woods are often the habitat of monsters and evil spiritual beings, but the word "demons" sometimes describes destructive forces within ourselves. Terms like "beasts" and "demons" may describe addictions to certain substances or behaviours, an inclination toward anger and violence, or a possession by anxiety, depression, or fear itself. You may know these tendencies in yourself only too well. There may have been times when you have responded to a certain situation in a way that surprises and alarms you. You may not have known that you were capable of such feelings or actions. You may even have said, "I scared myself."

It is curious that in our post-Enlightenment era, people have returned to using the term "demon" to describe destructive tendencies in themselves. Whether or not we think of these beings—as people of biblical and other cultures have—in literal terms, the demonic element in our personalities is something that many of us can recognize. There is something inside that threatens to disintegrate the components of our being and undo our attempts to gain health and wholeness. We sometimes seem to be our own worst enemies.

It is important to be able to acknowledge and name this untamed wildness in ourselves and to recognize when it threatens to be truly destructive for ourselves and those around us. It may not always be possible to exorcise the demon or vanquish the inner beast. But through self-awareness, counselling and support, and faith in a greater power, many have found ways of checking these harmful forces.

That said, not all the wildness in us is meant to be domesticated. Some philosophies look askance at human passion and take the attitude that our object in life should be to subdue all that is passionate in us. Passion in the form of angry outbursts or sexual aggression may well be something that humanity would be better off without. But a deep commitment to social justice or to the health of the environment can be described as a passion as well, and humanity would be poorer without passions like these. In the same sense, humanity would be poorer if none of us noticed what is wrong with the world and we all accommodated ourselves to things as they are. One meaning of "passion" has to do with a capacity to feel. It is in that sense that it is used to describe the last days of Jesus' life, when what he felt was suffering. Not insignificantly, it is in those last days that the first three gospels place one of Jesus' most passionate acts: the cleansing of the temple. Driving out the money-changers was an act of wildness, passion, and righteous indignation.

The wildness inside may frighten and alarm us with its destructive potential. But it can have a creative side as well. It may have the capacity to drive out the things that are false or shallow and clear the way for what is honest, profound, and true. In such a way, a wild man named John the Baptist railed against human wrong and prepared the way for a new order of things. Rather than being subdued or neutralized, some wildness is meant to be directed into life-giving channels. Who would want to see little Max's wildness eradicated? Would you not rather see it developed into a passion for life?

For personal reflection or group discussion

1. Think of something that you feared more at an earlier stage of your life than you do now. Is there anything that you fear more now than you did when you were younger? What has happened to change your feelings about these things?

2. Have you ever felt really passionate about something? Do you still feel that passion or have you lost it? Why? In your experience, does passion have a "downside"?

3. At this point in your life, is fear of something diminishing you in some way— holding you back from doing something you would like to do or limiting your freedom to act? Can you see a way of moving through that fear? Can you identify any allies or resources that might help you?

chapter 7

in a forest dark
embracing the shadow

On a sunny day late in the fall, I was walking in a ravine through a forest that I knew well. After crossing and recrossing the stream that ran through this gorge, I came at last to my favourite part of the woods. Here deciduous trees that had lost their leaves—trembling aspens and white paper birch—gave way to black spruce and other evergreens. When our children were small, I had called this the Storybook Woods because it reminded me of illustrations in books their mother and I read to them. There was little ground cover, just tree trunks widely separated, with branches starting well above the ground and providing a shady canopy that made these woods seem dark, remote, and mysterious compared with the rest of the forest. Even on this sunny day, it was a place of marked contrast between light and shadow.

DANTE SETS THE DIVINE COMEDY "in a forest dark," understood as a place of moral chaos and alienation from God, where the darkness of the woods represents sin and error. The previous chapter considered the forest as a mysterious and fearful place. Forests like these are often depicted as dark places where danger lurks in the shadows.

Darkness itself can be an object of fear—for children, but also for adults. A few years ago, I stayed with my family at a fairly primitive hostel in the forests of the Rocky Mountains. When I woke in the night, it was to pitch darkness. I could see nothing in the room around my bunk. I could not see the bunk itself, or my hand in front of my face. I could hardly tell which way was up. I had to keep a sense of panic from rising within me and overwhelming me. Since that night, if I were asked the familiar question, "Are you afraid of the dark?" I would have to honestly answer, "yes."

Although these associations are called into question by concerns about racial justice—a subject to which this chapter will return—there is a strong tradition in Western culture that uses darkness as a symbol of negative things. A play or movie described as "dark" explores the more sinister aspects of human nature. "Black" humour has a grim edge to it. Dante associated darkness with spiritual and moral confusion. Stories set in a forest often include the warning that one should get out of the woods before dark. And when darkness makes an appearance in scripture, it is often cast—to make a play on words—in a negative light.

Light and Darkness in Scripture and Christian Tradition

Biblically speaking, the equations are simple and easy to understand: light equals good; darkness equals bad. They are there from the very first chapter of Genesis. "Darkness covered the face of the deep.... Then God said, 'Let there be light'; and there was light. And God saw that the light was good; and God separated the light from the darkness" (Genesis 1:2–3).

The psalmist knows how it feels to stumble around in the dark and to long for a light to guide him. To God he says, "Your word is a lamp to my feet and a light to my path" (Psalm 119:105).

Matthew's gospel describes Jesus' followers as the light of the world in the Sermon on the Mount, where Jesus admonishes them not to hide their light under a bushel. In John's gospel Jesus himself is described as the light of the world who experienced rejection. "The light has come into the world, and people loved darkness rather than light because their deeds were evil. For all who do evil hate the light and do not come to the light, so that their deeds may not be exposed" (John 3:19–20).

Paul, in the letters of the New Testament, counsels his readers to "lay aside the works of darkness and put on the armor of light" (Romans 13:12). The author of Ephesians writes to the Christian community at Ephesus: "Once you were darkness, but now in the Lord you are light. Live as children of light" (Ephesians 5:8). The writer of the First Letter of Peter reminds correspondents that God has called them "out of darkness into his marvelous light" (1 Peter 2:9). But nowhere is the contrast more stark than in the First Letter of John: "God is light and in him there is no darkness at all" (1 John 1:5).

In view of passages like these—and many more—it is not surprising that among the names ascribed to the devil by Christian tradition is Prince of Darkness. Nor that so many familiar hymns pick up on the theme of light versus darkness. "Let There Be Light," "Jesus Bids Us Shine," "This Little Light of Mine," "In the Darkness Shines the Splendour," "Lead, Kindly Light (amid the encircling gloom)": innumerable hymns use light as a positive image, brought into even sharper relief by the surrounding darkness.

But beyond identifying light as a positive image and darkness as a negative one, what contrasting pairs do these images suggest? In scripture and Christian tradition—and in Western culture generally—the symbolism may be varied, but it is always easy to understand. At a fairly literal level, light suggests illumination, enlightenment, and knowledge, while darkness stands for ignorance—especially spiritual and moral ignorance. Light represents righteousness and godliness, while darkness symbolizes sin and evil. Where light stands for truth, darkness represents falsehood.

In other contexts, dark shadows are places for secrets, lies, and shameful activities—the things one tries to hide that may be revealed in the harsh light of day. As a radio program famously put it, it is the Shadow who knows the evil that lurks in the hearts of men. Fear of exposure may lead one to stay hidden in a forest dark.

Light—a "kindly light"—may suggest warmth. By way of contrast, I recall when certain Albertans told Ontarians that they were welcome to freeze in the dark. Light as a source of faith and comfort in the darkness of fear is suggested in a line from "The Servant Song," a well-loved hymn. The singers assure one another, "I will hold the Christ-light for you in the night-time of your fear."[1] Another hymn, "Joyful, Joyful We Adore You," asks God to "drive the gloom of doubt away." The darkness of doubt is contrasted with the light of faith.

Redeeming an Image

In the pairs evoked by the ideas of light and darkness, darkness always seems to represent something negative. You may wonder whether anything good can be said about dark shadows at all. But when God divided the light from the darkness, was not the darkness also good? It is important to be aware of recent efforts to redeem the idea of darkness. There are good reasons for taking a second look at the symbolism associated with darkness and to discern positive associations that have been overlooked.

Another image drawn from the forest can help show that some things we are quick to dismiss as irredeemably destructive can have a positive aspect. Since biblical times, the forest fire (ironically, an image of light) has evoked images of devastation. No one familiar with the idea of hellfire will be surprised to learn that forest fires are sometimes seen in the Hebrew scriptures as a sign of God's judgment. In an oracle that threatens the complacent but unfaithful people of Jerusalem, Jeremiah imagines God declaring, "I will kindle a fire in its forest"—a likely reference to the palace built of cedar known as the House of the Forest of the Lebanon—"and it shall devour all that is around it" (Jeremiah 21:14). And in Isaiah, the people's wickedness itself is compared to a forest fire:

For wickedness burned like a fire,
consuming briers and thorns;
it kindled the thickets of the forest,
and they swirled upward in a column of smoke. (Isaiah 9:18)

The Old Testament prophets used the forest fire as a very negative image. But in our own day we are exposed to facts that help us to see forest fires not merely as negative forces.

Hikers who walk the Falcon Creek Self-Guiding Trail in Manitoba's Whiteshell Provincial Park are invited to take along a brochure to help them understand what they are seeing. It is written as a dialogue between a fictional cottager and an old prospector who once worked a mine in the area. The two characters come to a clearing of 18 hectares destroyed in 1981 by a forest fire. They agree in condemning the careless human act that caused this particular fire. But the cottager has something to add. He tells the old-timer that despite the destruction, there can be a positive side to natural or controlled fires. The burning of dead vegetation makes the soil more fertile, allowing new growth that returning animals feed on. And jack pine cones open and release their seeds only in the kind of extreme heat associated with a fire.

Thus forest fires, which can be so destructive, can also promote a forest's renewal. Fires can clean out deadfall, create meadows, increase growth of diverse vegetation, and clear new passageways for animals. In fact, the risk of a later, more catastrophic fire can be reduced by an earlier, less major one. It brings to mind an expression of the medieval mystic Meister Eckhart: growth by subtraction.

Because forest fires that make the news are those that do major, unwanted damage, we may lose sight of the fact that something so bad can sometimes also be good. Similarly, because of the negative ways in which the idea of darkness has been used as metaphor, we need to be reminded that it, too, is an image that deserves another look.

What is wrong with using "darkness" as a consistently negative image? Recently, I have become increasingly sensitive to the racial overtones that negative images of darkness can carry. Light and dark, white and black—when we equate these pairings with good and bad, it is easy to see that they are problematic. What did it mean when Europeans in the 19th and 20th centuries referred to Africa as "the dark continent" when Africa saw more sunlight hours than Europe? None of the connotations that come immediately to mind seem positive. "Dark" in this instance suggested a dense jungle—a forest dark—where the light of "civilization" had never penetrated. It implied that, to Europeans at least, this part of the world was unknown, undeveloped, and mysterious. Could it be entirely coincidental that "dark" also describes the skin tones of most sub-Saharan Africans?

Concerns about these connotations is one motivation for re-examining our feelings about darkness. Some Christian writers and liturgists have responded by searching for other images to represent positive and negative aspects of life—ways that abandon talk of light and darkness entirely. Others, though, have begun to identify ways in which darkness can be a positive image.

In scripture, wild animals are often seen as threatening and harmful. But a verse from the psalms reminds us of God's care for the needs of wild animals and of the fact that darkness, no less than light, has a place in the providence of God. "You make darkness, and it is night, when all the animals of the forest come creeping out" (Psalm 104:20).

Consider also that we spend the nine months of our gestation "where the sun don't shine." It is warm, protective, and nourishing; the dark is a place where we grow. The writer of Psalm 139 praises God for making him in secret, intricately woven in his mother's womb, "fearfully and wonderfully made" (139:14).

Darkness suggests protection in other psalms. In Psalm 17, for example, the poet prays to God, "hide me in the shadow of your wings" (17:8*b*). Psalm 36, using the same image, affirms "all people may take refuge in the shadow of your wings" (36:7). When Psalm 121 describes God as "your shade at your right hand" (121:5), this metaphor would have been particularly meaningful to a people who were otherwise exposed to the relentless heat of the sun in a treeless landscape. Today, migraine sufferers who achieve a measure of relief only in darkness may find such an image effective.

If darkness can evoke refuge and relief, coolness and protection, it can also suggest quiet and a slower pace. Fast food outlets keep customers moving with bright lighting and loud, lively music. Restaurants that want to encourage leisurely dining provide a quieter setting with "mood lighting." Their ambience provides respite from stress by creating a darker, quieter environment than most of the places where we work and live. Similarly, the places where people go for a therapeutic massage are likely to have more subdued lighting than the stressful world outside.

At times, an enfolding darkness may suggest solitude and comfort. At least these qualities are inherent in the mood conveyed by Robert Frost's poem "Stopping by Woods on a Snowy Evening." In describing the woods, Frost places the adjective "dark" between two others: "lovely" and "deep."

Joan Cannon Borton records similar positive associations with darkness. A mental health counsellor and Benedictine oblate, Borton finds replenishment and space for reflection in the stillness and solitude of the dark. In fact, the positive qualities associated with darkness—coolness, relief, refuge, quiet, solitude—are all qualities that people may associate with a walk in the woods, or in a forest dark.

Embracing the Darkness

Notwithstanding what has been said in praise of darkness, in biblical and Western traditions it has been used more often as a negative image. Hymns like Brian Wren's "Joyful Is the Dark" are far outnumbered by hymns extolling the virtues of light. Yet even though darkness may most often represent negative things, there are times when it is appropriate to embrace that darkness.

The familiar phrase "the dark night of the soul" is likely to evoke negative associations. It originated as the title of a book by the medieval mystic St. John of the Cross. The expression has found its way into our language to describe a period of anxiety or depression, a spiritual crisis, or an episode of suffering. The phrase evokes an unpleasant experience that one may be inclined to avoid, and yet that may ultimately be inescapable.

I once belonged to a men's discussion group that met over a period of years. Several men in the group had experienced depression. On more than one occasion we talked about whether to do everything we could to resist depression—to regard it as an unnatural experience that should be treated medically—or whether there may be times when we simply need to give ourselves to it and let it have its time with us. Some physical wounds need to be given time to heal; the same may be true of psychic wounds as well.

In her book *Soul Maps: A Guide to the Mid-life Spirit*, Mardi Tindal recalls a conversation with a university instructor named Susan. It is through the darker experiences of life, Susan thinks, that we are sometimes called to something new. Fear can be one of these darker experiences. But Susan adds, "I think illness, depression, interpersonal breakdown, and vocational crises provide times for breakthrough—as when there's that thin sheaf or line between darkness and daylight when things begin shifting and one becomes aware that there's something else out there."[2]

Another of Mardi Tindal's conversations was with Lynn, a woman for whom grief had been the darkness to which she had given herself and in which she had found transformation. Lynn's son had committed suicide. Those of us who have not experienced such tragic loss in our lives can hardly imagine how radically her life had been changed by this event. Lynn eventually discovered a new sense of direction in her life and a new sense of what she had to give. But that came only after she embraced the darkness. Every night for a year, she said, she read a prayer that begins, "When sorrow comes, let us accept it simply, as a part of life. Let the heart be open to pain; let it be stretched by it."[3]

There is a delicate balance here, of course. People can become mired in the darkness of grief, depression, or some other personal crisis. Those who have honoured the place of darkness in their lives rarely speak of it as a destination or as something to be indulged indefinitely. Rather they see it as something to be embraced for a time, to be given its due. It is understood as a "dark passage" leading to somewhere else.

Me and My Shadow

In speaking of the son who had died, Lynn refers to him as her "shadow child," an expression that evokes his presence with her. The image of shadow—our own shadow—is reflected in common sayings ("He's afraid of his own shadow"; "She's a shadow of her former self"), in poems (Robert Louis Stevenson's "I Have a Little Shadow"), in songs ("Me and My Shadow"), and in plays (Peter Pan keeps his shadow in a drawer). Perhaps most significantly, it is a theme of the writings of pioneer psychologist Carl Jung.

The 23rd Psalm's reference to "the valley of the shadow" (in the *King James Version*) may suggest shadow as an aspect of the environment around us, as a way of experiencing the external circumstances in which we sometimes find ourselves. But just as wildness is both something that can threaten us from without and something that we can discover within ourselves, shadowlands may be found not only in the world around us but within our own psyches. And just as in the world, light inevitably casts shadows, there is an inevitability about the duality of light and shadow within ourselves. However faint or sketchy they may be, our shadows are things we cannot shake. As Stevenson says in his poem, they go in and out with us.

As with darkness itself, it may be common to understand shadows as a negative image. Speaking of a person's "dark side" or "shadow side" may refer to something evil or destructive in his or her personality. "Shadow" may describe aspects of your personality that you try to deny because you do not regard them as being very attractive. You may understand your shadow to represent unexpressed emotions that are at odds with the persona that you like to show the world. Indeed, it is possible at times in reading Jung and those who have come after him to form the impression that the "shadow" refers merely to negative aspects of character—to a tendency to sabotage one's relationships, for example, or to play the role of martyr.

But it is also possible to understand the shadow as any aspect of yourself that seeks acknowledgement and self-acceptance, assimilation and expression if you are to be a fully human, three-dimensional person. A familiar idea is that men, who may define themselves in terms of masculinity, also have a feminine side (*anima*), while women, who may be conscious of the things that make them female, also have a masculine side (*animus*). But beyond that there are shadows that are specific to each one of us. One person's shadow may include a neglected talent as an artist or musician. For another it may include a positive character trait that has yet to be called upon and that seeks an opportunity for expression. For another it may revolve around a dream of what might have been—and may yet be. Unacknowledged and frustrated, our shadows may indeed be projected in negative and destructive ways onto other people. Recognized as part of ourselves, they may be expressed in ways that are healthy and creative for us and helpful for others.

The ultimate shadow of human existence—and the hardest to accept—is death. In fact, the "valley of the shadow" of Psalm 23 refers to the "shadow of death." Our mortality may be a distant backdrop to our daily lives until we find ourselves walking through that valley. But sooner or later we will all find ourselves there. Since religions deal with ultimate things, it is not surprising that many include ritualistic re-enactments of death. Christian baptism, for instance—at least when it takes the form of immersion—parallels dying and rising with Christ. And in some rites of initiation, the candidate would symbolically face death by being left, abandoned and alone for a time, in a dark forest.

Light and shadow, life and death, masculine and feminine, faith and doubt: it is natural, at times, to think in terms of dualities. But one side of the duality does not have a monopoly on all that is positive and needful. Each side has its part to play.

A woman I know has lost the sight in one eye. She no longer drives at night, but she does during the day. I asked her what she does about depth perception. The shadows help, she said. The shadows help to give her perspective a third dimension. They prevent the landscape from appearing flat and featureless. They help her to see where she is going.

For personal reflection or group discussion

1. Try sitting silently in the dark for 10 minutes. Did you find this a positive or a negative experience—or neither, or both? Why?

2. Have you gone through what you would call a "dark" time in your life? What made it dark? Did you find yourself resisting or embracing the darkness? Were you changed by the experience?

3. A person's shadow can include undeveloped talents or character traits that seek expression. Can you name one or more of these things for you?

chapter 8

sometimes people leave you
partings and loss

We did it as a kind of experiment. A friend and I went for a walk in the forest. Partway through our walk my friend left me and retraced his steps, while I went on alone. In the minutes that followed, I found myself continuing our conversation inside my head. I would notice something that I might have pointed out to him if he had been there, but then remember that he was no longer with me to share this experience. At other times, I would be aware that I no longer needed to consult with him about where to go or what to do next. I was free to make my own decisions as I continued to make my solitary way through these unfamiliar woods.

AT THE END OF ACT I of the musical *Into the Woods*, it seems that everything has been sorted out. The fairy-tale characters who have gone into the woods in search of something have all been successful in their quests. Cinderella and her Prince have found each other. The Baker and his Wife have their longed-for child. Jack (of "Jack and the Beanstalk") and his Mother are no longer poor; in fact, they are set for life. After their nasty encounters with the Wolf, Little Red Ridinghood and her Grandmother have killed the beast and emerged to live happily ever after. It seems like the end of the story.

But, although in life there are said to be no second acts, in this musical there is one. All the things that came together in Act I start to come apart. In the great unravelling that is Act II, Cinderella's Prince strays in pursuit of other women, including Sleeping Beauty and the Baker's Wife. The Prince's Steward kills Jack's Mother. A giant dispatches the Baker's Wife and destroys Little Red Ridinghood's house, killing her Mother. We learn that Little Red Ridinghood's Grandmother, too, is missing. As the play nears its conclusion, Cinderella sings a song to Little Red Ridinghood called "No One Is Alone." "Sometimes people leave you," she sings, "Halfway through the wood."[1] The Baker and Jack join in, as the four characters—who have each sustained a major loss—try to face the harsh reality and comfort one another.

Our close relationships help to define us and give spiritual shape to our lives. These relationships are among the things that make us human.

However, many of our most important relationships do not last a lifetime. Sometimes, in one way or another, people leave us halfway—or at least part-way—through the woods. Some of these "leavings" are unexpected and shock-ing. But even those that are part of the natural evolution of a life can have painful, far-reaching consequences.

Stories that involve parting and the prospect of being left alone can be poignant and powerful. Traditional fairy tales—like the ones to which the Sondheim/Lapine musical refers—can evoke separation anxieties and fears of abandonment that originate in childhood. And often in these stories, the setting for such separation and abandonment is a forest.

Typically in these tales, events are triggered by a change of circumstances that undermines things that had been taken for granted. These things can no longer be counted on; the change may, for example, render a home no longer a safe and secure place. A child's beloved parent dies, to be replaced by a step-parent who has no regard for the child. An economic reversal leaves a family with too many mouths to feed. Children are taken deep into the woods and

abandoned there. The soft-heartedness of a parent and the appealing innocence of children may be equally ineffective in resisting such a turn of events.

In real life, too, you may find that your resources are powerless to stop
people from leaving.

Partings That We Expect

One can sometimes be philosophical about partings that are seen as part of
the cycle of life.

The second chapter of Genesis says that this cycle includes a man leaving
his father and mother to be joined to his wife (Genesis 2:24). But in today's
culture, marriage is not the only occasion for the next generation to leave the
parental home. In fact, it has become relatively rare in North America for
young people to move directly from the home in which they were raised into
the home they will share with a spouse. More often a young adult will live alone
or with friends before taking the next step—and that next step may well involve
a live-in relationship with the person who will eventually become a spouse.

Leaving home can also involve a false start or two. A failed relationship, the
loss of a job, or a decision to pursue further education can send adult children
back to the parental nest. Back at home, the relationship must be renegotiated
between the parents and an adult child who has tasted independence.

But with all of the cultural variables of time and place, leaving home continues to be a rite of passage. And like other rites of passage, it is accompanied
by emotions and adjustments. Even if the predominant emotion on the part
of both parent and child is relief, that relief may be tinged with something
wistful. Although life is supposed to unfold this way, you may still find yourself "filling up" emotionally at the realization that for each of the players, one
chapter is ending and another beginning. That is why graduations and wed-
dings—essentially happy occasions—are often accompanied by tears.

A ritual lasts only a few moments, but the reality it marks may come about
more gradually. The ritual represents a shifting in a relationship that may have
gone on for years and that will continue to evolve. When the ritual is about
leaving home or coming of age, it marks a change of relationship between
parent and child. The child becomes an adult and a different understanding of the relationship between parent and child is appropriate. This adjust-
ment is not always easy. In *Into the Woods*, Rapunzel's mother expresses her
difficulty in letting go of a child who is ready to see the world. In the song
"Stay with Me," we hear both a mother's desire to protect her child from a

dark, wild world, and that same mother's self-pitying attempts to keep her child in a dependent relationship.

Another natural, expected, but not necessarily easy parting is the death of your parents in old age. When a parent dies, you may feel surprised and not surprised at the same time. It was bound to happen sometime, but it may still catch you unprepared when it does.

Depending on the circumstances, a parent's death can produce feelings of shock, regret, anger, confusion, relief, guilt—all of the feelings that go together to make up "grief." What has been lost? In missing this person, you miss particular things. It might be a source of guidance that you miss—or a place to talk over a problem. It might be the sense of continuity provided by someone who could remember your childhood and who was a connection to previous generations. If it was a troubled relationship, the patterns of the conflict may have provided at least a strange sense of familiarity; and now that is gone. If the relationship was more benign, the loss may be of one less person in the world who loves you.

The death of a parent brings up more than the emotions associated with other losses. It often brings up questions of identity and relationship as well. As parents age, their children's relationships with them continue to evolve. Often people end up caring for those who once cared for them. Such changes can bring a gradual shift in one's sense of identity, and that shift may not go smoothly. The change continues when first one parent and then the other dies. If you once identified yourself—or even defined yourself—as someone's son or daughter, that aspect of your identity is, in a certain sense, gone. Yet, you may find that there is work left to do in coming to terms with who you are in relation to your parents.

Unexpected Partings

In addition to the partings that can be seen as natural and anticipated, people leave us in unexpected ways. A parent—or a spouse, sibling, or friend—may unexpectedly die. A married couple may live with an unspoken assumption about which of them will likely die first, but find that events unfold in another way. Life can be challenging enough when things work out as expected. It is challenging in a different way when things turn out to confound expectations.

When a child dies before his or her parent, for example, it may seem contrary not only to what is natural but to what is just and fair. Things like this happen, but the injustice may hit home only when they touch *you*. You may find yourself feeling angry at the person who has left, or angry at God. What a funeral prayer calls "the shortness and uncertainty of human life" may shake your assumptions about life and about the way the world is supposed to work. Things you had counted on for a sense of security and meaning may not be as solid as you had imagined.

Not all partings involve death, of course. Relationships can come to an end by people leaving physically or emotionally, through alienation or simple neglect.

You may live in the same town or city as a good friend for years, never expecting geography to divide you. But that friend moves away, and despite your best intentions the closeness of the relationship declines.

Some find that people they have felt close to through their work fade away when they change jobs or retire. Some are disillusioned to find that people they thought of as friends disappear when they are beset by a serious illness, a change in marital status, or some other reversal in their lives. A sense of abandonment can undermine your confidence in the appearance of things and bring home the fragility not only of human life but of human relationships.

The ending of a marriage is a particularly difficult parting. Few people who get married are cynical enough to do so expecting their marriage to fail. But we all know the statistics. A large percentage of marriages do come to an end.

Sometimes one partner leaves even when the other would like the relationship to continue. Or the ending comes about by mutual agreement, although even then at least one partner will physically leave the home the couple has shared. Often one or both partners have already "left" emotionally long before the separation takes place. And if anger, guilt, resentment, confusion, and all the other aspects of grief can accompany the death of a person, they can certainly accompany the death of a marriage.

The death of a significant person in your life can raise questions about what sort of person you are and about the ways in which your relationships define you. Separation and divorce can do all that, too—and add questions of self-worth, as well.

Challenge and Response

A parting may be expected or unexpected, sudden or gradual, through a change of location or a change of heart, through a death or a human decision. But no life is without its experiences of people leaving—and taking things with them.

For those who are left behind, these experiences draw a variety of emotional reactions. Each one has significance—sometimes far-reaching and multi-faceted significance. And each one elicits a response. Losses like these are sometimes said to build character. But more accurately, through our responses to them, we reveal and discover things about ourselves: what we are made of and what we are capable of.

An ending can lead you to become either more or less engaged in life. For some, the pain of loss leads to disengagement. You may feel that emotional investment in another will only lead to hurt when that person "leaves"—by dying or by withdrawing. So in a kind of pre-emptive action, you avoid the possibility of future pain by withdrawing first. You avoid getting too close to people. You find meaning in your work rather than in your relationships. You relate to many people but only at a superficial level. Or you may grow cynical about human relationships in general.

On the other hand, you may respond to a "leaving" by becoming more engaged in the relationships that remain. A divorced parent focuses more intentionally on raising his or her children and strengthening the relationships with them. A couple who, after focusing for years on raising a family, have become empty-nesters turn their attention to each other. They become intentional about re-inventing their relationship. A bereaved sibling comes to value a spousal relationship more highly.

In mid-life, a man I know suffered the sudden loss of his brother. He travelled to the funeral alone. His wife told me that the night after he returned home, when they went to bed, he hung on to her as if for dear life. His experience of the "shortness and uncertainty of human life" had drawn him closer to her.

Becoming more engaged in response to a loss can take the form of reconnecting with people from your past. After their parents have died, adult siblings often initiate more frequent contact with one another than they have had for some time. They are connecting with people who have known them all their lives and can remind them of some aspect of who they are. For some people, the death of a parent triggers an interest in family history. Researching your origins is a way of addressing the need for a sense of identity that has been challenged by the parent leaving.

A loss can spur people to connect in other ways. If you recognize your need to be a spiritual one, you may find yourself returning to a church or religious community. It may or may not be a spiritual community from your past, but your search for connection will reflect a new—or renewed—awareness of a spiritual need. You might pursue a similar need by seeking out a counsellor who can help to guide you through the emotions and questions that someone leaving has raised.

One way or another, many people come to see that they have been left with work to do. In *Into the Woods*, the Mysterious Man speaks for all fathers when he says to his son, "We die but we don't."[2] And in a reprise of the song "No One Is Alone," the Baker's Wife returns from the dead to assure the Baker that no one leaves for good. Even when people close to you die, they leave behind—for good or ill—a legacy to be dealt with.

The legacy left by a loved one may include things for which you are grateful: a good start in life, inherited talents, modelled values. But few legacies are without their complications. The men's group mentioned in the previous chapter devoted many hours to discussing our relationships with our fathers. That the fathers of some group members had died did not exempt them from coming to terms with how that relationship continued to shape them. It still affected their feelings of self-worth and influenced the way they tried to parent their own children. Some men found themselves still trying to win a parent's—even a dead parent's—approval.

The challenge is to respond to the experience of separation, and the work it has left to be done, by learning something. When people respond to the question "What have you learned?" with "I have learned that men are pigs" or "I don't seem to be relationship material," the answer indicates a need to continue working and to dig deeper. There is more to learn about other people, and more to learn about themselves.

Even qualities that you regard as virtues may have undermined a relationship. Recognizing this requires an ability to understand the subtleties of at least two personalities. And coming to terms with a self-image that is not as perfect as you would have liked to believe is not an easy task. It requires time and grace to accept responsibility for your own contribution to a destructive dynamic. And to forgive yourself and grow out of your past experiences requires trusting that in some ultimate sense, you are worthy of love and hope.

Following a separation, you may discover resources you didn't realize you had. These resources are drawn upon when you no longer have the other person to lean on. Although this relationship may have helped to define you, other aspects of your identity are independent of that relationship and deserve to be recognized. These learnings may help you to emerge from a difficult period of life not merely sadder but wiser. A bit of distance may not only provide a new perspective on a relationship that has ended or changed; it can also prepare you for the challenges of life's next chapter.

When You Are the One Who Leaves

A passage from the third chapter of the Book of Ecclesiastes is familiar to many people of my generation, if only from a musical setting of the words sung by the rock group the Byrds. It begins "For everything there is a season." A familiar list of contrasting times follows—a time to be born, and a time to die; a time to weep, and a time to laugh; and so on.

Some might add a time to stay, and a time to leave: many people have found themselves to be the ones who decide to leave home or to leave a relationship.

And ultimately, there is a time to die—a time for each of us to leave this world. Progress in medical science gives us more say than we used to have about when to make that final exit—a development that is fraught with ethical problems. But whether or not the time to leave this life is ours to choose, there are certainly times when we have to discern whether it is time to leave a particular situation.

You may have had to discern whether it was time to leave one job and consider another. Perhaps you asked yourself questions: "Have I done all I can do here?" "Is this organization entering a phase in which a different kind of leadership, skill, or talent will be required?" "Have I become stale, or do I still have something to offer?"

Young adults have to discern when it is time to stay in the family home and when it is time to go. Again there are questions: "Do I have the financial resources to make it on my own?" "Am I needed to stay and help out at home?" "Does increasing conflict with my parents mean that I need my own space?" And parents may need to discern when to give their children time to figure it out for themselves and when to give them a push.

A decision to leave a marriage—whether it is made by one or both partners—is often resisted. It can feel as if they are saying that investing so much of themselves in the relationship was a big mistake, and that they have wasted a significant part of their lives. At this point, the partners have yet to do the work that will help them see that their marriage is not merely something to be regretted or put behind them. When a decision is made to end a marriage, it may not yet be apparent that the relationship will always remain a significant expression of who the partners were at the time, and has helped to shape the people they will be.

Deciding to leave a marriage can also be difficult because the decision affects others, including people who have very little say in the matter. Even when it is clear to both partners that continuing the marriage is preventing them from being the people they were meant to be, leaving the relationship can be accompanied by feelings of guilt and failure. Family members may apply pressure to stay in the marriage (often "for the sake of the children") even when the couple knows that the marriage can no longer give life to those who are in it and around it. Married friends may communicate that the couple is "letting the side down." When others leave you, you may feel abandoned; if you are the one leaving, you may well feel guilt.

Other relationships are also difficult to leave. I once worked with someone who was good at pushing all my buttons. She played effectively on my need to be liked, to succeed where others had failed, and to not give up. Ultimately I recognized another need: the need for help in disengaging myself from this relationship. But the end of this relationship was also a wake-up call to seek a deeper kind of help—help in understanding why I needed all these things and how I could avoid this kind of jam in the future. There was an opportunity here, and the opportunity would have been lost if I had settled for a band-aid treatment that ignored the deeper problem.

Eventually, each one of us will leave this life. We may have some say in when that departure is made, or we may not. We may or may not have some warning of death's approach. However it happens, each scenario brings its own challenges and its own blessings.

A colleague of mine once recounted an experience that left a significant impression on her. She had just entered an elevator in an apartment building when she saw an elderly man approaching, laden with bags of groceries. She held the door for him. "Thanks," he said. "My wife told me that would happen." She had to ask what he meant. Well, he said, his wife had been diagnosed with a terminal illness. Theirs had been a traditional marriage with a division of labour in which she had done all the cooking and the housework. Realizing that her time was short, she applied herself to teaching him how to do the household chores that had always been her province. But she added, "Don't worry. You won't have to do everything by yourself. People will help you."

Whether you are given clues as to the day or the hour of your death or not, there are opportunities to consider the legacy you will leave to those who come after. You will do a good job—or a not-so-good job—of equipping them to continue their walk through the woods after you have to leave. And in claiming that legacy they will discover the truth spoken by the Baker's Wife: No one leaves for good.

For personal reflection or group discussion

1. Think of a person who has left you by dying. What emotions did their leaving evoke in you? In what ways have you come to terms (or not) with their leaving?

2. Think of a relationship in your life (e.g., a marriage, a friendship) that has ended. Who left? What have you been left with?

3. What intangible legacy would you like to leave those who come after you? What have you done to ensure that they will receive this legacy?

chapter 9

in another part of the forest
beyond the mainstream

I had been in these urban woods before, but on this visit I decided to take a different path and explore an unfamiliar area. It was with a sense of anticipation, curiosity, and adventure that I set off down the trail. As near as it was to the part of the woods I had visited previously, this area seemed different in some respects. The air felt cooler; the canopy of leaves and branches looked thicker. At a farther remove from the sounds of humanity, the song-birds here seemed more plentiful. In the more familiar part of the woods, I had been used to encountering other walkers. But in this more remote area, I found myself walking a good part of my hour-long route without seeing another soul.

IN CHOOSING A SETTING for the play *As You Like It*, Shakespeare thought back to the countryside around his native Stratford-upon-Avon. The Forest of Arden seems to have been based on a forest near Shakespeare's hometown—a forest that would have been familiar to him in his youth. In this comedy, city dwellers find themselves in the woods, where they get caught up in a series of complications involving usurped authority, exile, frustrated love, and gender confusion. The forest must have been of considerable size to accommodate the various encounters among the characters. In fact, in order to distinguish its setting from that of the previous scene, one scene is headed with the stage direction "Another part of the forest."

Giving their anthology of shorter gay fiction the title *Meanwhile, in Another Part of the Forest*, Alberto Manguel and Craig Stephenson had more than a Shakespearean allusion in mind. In the introduction to this collection, Manguel refers to the intriguing line that would often appear at the top of a panel in the comic books he read in his youth. The words "meanwhile, in another part of the forest …" suggested that you could know what happened on a mysterious fork in the road that had not been taken or was less apparent, and that led to other adventures.

A collection of gay fiction represents a variety of human experience that might not be considered a part of the mainstream. This chapter invites you to reflect on aspects of your own life that are not part of the social or cultural mainstream in which most people live. It is also an opportunity to think about aspects of your life that are not part of your *own* mainstream, and about periods of your life that seem remote from your present situation. Thus, the expression "another part of the forest" can be applied to your past, your present, and your future.

Other Parts of the Forest: Past Tense

Art historian Kenneth Clark was just past 70 when he wrote the first volume of his autobiography. It accounted for almost exactly the first half of his life to that point, taking him to the age of 36. Recalling a period that seemed remote from his present existence, he deliberately borrowed from Dante and Shakespeare in giving this volume the title *Another Part of the Wood*.

When something prompts you to revisit an earlier chapter of your life, it can feel like another part of the forest, a place where you once lived but live no longer. Things may have been so different then that you hardly recognize the earlier self who lived there. Yet making contact with that earlier self can help you understand the person you have become. That other part of the forest does have a connection with the part you live in now.

What sorts of experiences may prompt a visit—an imaginative visit or a literal one—to a part of the forest where you once lived? In the past couple of years, I have had a number of experiences, with different "triggers," that brought me into contact with earlier chapters of my life.

When my aunt died on the West Coast, I was asked to speak at her memorial service. This gave me an opportunity to revisit a community where I had lived for four years as a boy. The service took place in the church where my father had been minister. Afterwards my brother and I walked along the creek in the woods nearby where we had played as boys. Our conversation prompted memories of people and events we had hardly thought about in the intervening years.

Last year I happened to meet a man whom I had not seen since we were in junior high school. He had reconnected with another classmate, and I had recently bumped into yet another, so the four of us arranged to get together for lunch. It was a time to reminisce about things that had happened in our school days and bring an adult perspective to them, and to catch up on several decades of our lives. I learned about some of the hurts my classmates had sustained as boys—which we had been too proud or embarrassed to share with one another at the time. I learned, too, that none of us had survived the years that followed without disappointments.

The year I was born some relatives bought a house in Vancouver. In my extended family, no one lived longer in a single home than they did. But not long ago, the last member of that family died. The house was sold and, as so often happens, the new owners demolished it and built a much grander residence in its place. Shortly before the sale went through, I had an opportunity to drive past and take a picture of the home where so many family gatherings had taken place over the years. With a feeling of wistfulness, I had my last look at this link with my past.

These examples from my own life may evoke similar ones from yours. Various events can trigger a visit to a part of the woods that was known to you once but has become remote from your present existence. A wedding or a funeral, a family or school reunion, a phone call out of the blue from a childhood friend or a long-lost relative—such events may invite a visit to a past chapter of your life. In some cases, the visit is perfunctory. But some visits challenge you to reassess people or events from your past, or spark memories that help you understand how you became the person you are.

As my three school friends and I discovered when we had lunch that day, the passing of time can provide a different perspective on the past. We revealed things about ourselves that afternoon that helped us to understand what each of us had been experiencing in those far-off days. Each of us had pieces of information about our teachers and fellow-classmates that helped us to see them in a different light. These people were more complex beings than we had imagined them to be when we were young.

I have had similar experiences visiting with cousins and comparing notes on our parents and grandparents. In conversations like these, one person's memory can shed light on another's. Understanding may be gained about why people behaved the way they did, or what relationships in our own or previous generations of the family were really like. Sometimes there can be an "aha" moment as a piece of a puzzle is given a context and falls into place.

Visiting a part of the wood where you spent time in the past can also help you to understand yourself better. The distance between that part of the forest and the part you inhabit now has brought changes. Circumstances have changed, and so have you. Some of the changes may make you feel sad. You may feel that you were safer and more secure, that life was simpler and more innocent in this other part of the wood. Even if that impression is idealized or illusory—based more on what you wish had been than on what actually was— it may leave feelings of nostalgia. You may not only feel sad about what has been lost. You may also feel disappointed in yourself or resentful toward others if your journey since that time has not fulfilled the promise of earlier days.

Parts of the woods you have known in the past may also be painful places where you don't want to go. You may avoid situations where you have to confront the things you lived with there: abuse, rejection, neglect, poverty, illness, or injury. You may be glad to be free of the things that hurt or limited you. You have turned your back on that part of the woods, and refuse to go back even for a visit.

And yet, if as Tennyson's Ulysses claims we are a part of all that we have met, sooner or later you may find that these parts of the forest, however distant and remote you imagine them to be, continue to affect who you are. They continue to shape your values and explain your behaviours, to nag at you and demand your attention. Like it or not, from time to time the past has a way of poking its nose into the present.

If a part of the forest where you used to live was unpleasant for you, you may need companions—friends or professionals—to help you find your way when you revisit it and come to terms with what was and, to some degree, still is.

When a part of the woods that you once knew has left you with pleasant memories, you may face a different challenge. The four school friends who met for lunch spoke of getting together again. One even wanted to make it a regular event. But none of us should have been surprised when our enthusiasm for this idea quickly evaporated. We had gone in different directions since we had been together. To have tried to make something permanent out of this pleasant encounter would have been artificial. If another part of the forest was a good place to be, you may wish to visit it occasionally. But you can't live there. As an Irish song expresses it, "There is no future in the past."

Even Jesus discovered that "you can't go home again" (as Tom Wolfe's book title puts it). Jesus found it hard to go home even for a visit. The three synoptic gospels (Matthew, Mark, and Luke) all record the rough reception he received when, having begun his adult ministry, he returned to Nazareth, where he had spent his formative years. The hometown crowd was variously amazed and dismissive at the teaching of this carpenter's son from an ordinary family. They had seen him grow up in their midst; now they rejected him. Jesus, we are told, was not able to do many deeds of power there and soon went on his way. This was no longer a place where he could live and work. Even a visit brought disappointment. The future lay elsewhere.

Experiences like this notwithstanding, you may find that now-remote parts of the forest had a hand in shaping you. A brief visit can help you recognize and reclaim some aspect of yourself that had been ignored or rejected for years.

The first time I participated in a Myers-Briggs personality exercise, people who knew me through my work were surprised—and I was even a little surprised myself—to find that I scored higher on the F (for feeling) than on the T (for thinking) side of the ledger. But as I revisited my reactions to events in my childhood, I recognized that emotional responses were more evident than rational thinking. In the years since I left that part of the woods, I had learned to think analytically and to value logic. As I grew up, I may also have confused maturity (a desirable thing) with the suppression of emotions (an undesirable thing). My years at university had educated the F out of me! Imaginatively revisiting the part of the wood where I lived in my earlier years, I began to reclaim my earlier responses as a legitimate part of my adult self.

Other Parts of the Forest: Present Tense

In switching to the present tense, think of aspects of your life—as it is now—that may not fit into the mainstream of the society you live in or into the mainstream of your own life. The present tense may include work, relationships, or a pattern of living that has been in place for some time. It includes the part of the woods where you currently spend the greater share of your time and that forms the greater part of your consciousness. But it may also include parts of the forest that you visit occasionally, which are perhaps a bit strange, exotic, or remote from most people's experience. It can include aspects of your life that some people who know you reasonably well would find surprising.

At its simplest level, you might think of an interest, hobby, or avocation that takes you—either regularly or occasionally—into another part of the forest. An accountant plays in a jazz band on the weekends; a stay-at-home parent, on a slow-pitch team every spring. A schoolteacher flies a light plane in her spare time. Sometimes a person's pastime would surprise those whose relationship is limited to the part of the woods that they share. I had a passing acquaintance with a man for some years before I learned that he had an elaborate model railway in his basement. This hobby occupied much of his spare time, and connected him to a community of people quite different from those he encountered in the rest of his life.

Often the other part of the forest is a place that calls forth some talent or personality trait that is not evident in the mainstream of your life. It may give expression to something creative or funky, playful or silly that is not valued or endorsed in the part of your life where you spend the bulk of your time. You may even feel vaguely embarrassed or ashamed about devoting some of your time to what others do not regard as a very productive, sensible, or worthwhile activity. And yet this is a place where a significant part of your being finds an outlet.

The rhythm of the year can provide a place where another aspect of your being can receive the attention it needs. Some people who work in urban settings look forward to a vacation literally in the woods, camping or at a cottage. Here they find a different mode of being, a different pace of life. They find something that not only nourishes their souls but enables them to express aspects of their personalities that are stifled in the workplace.

You can also find yourself in another part of the forest through certain relationships. Some of us find our friendships with people who are much like ourselves, who share our background, who come from and continue to live in the same part of the woods as we do. But others are enriched by personal connections with people who come from quite a different part of the forest. When we are with them, they invite us to become acquainted with that other part of the forest ourselves.

Knowing people of other religions, races, socio-economic groups, ages, or sexual orientations can challenge your assumptions about reality and broaden your understanding of what makes people alike or different. If you marry or spend enough time with another person to meet his or her family, you will be introduced to ways of life that are different from your own. If your most significant connections are made with someone who comes from a very different background, you may find yourself—especially when you spend time with his or her side of the family—to be in a very different part of the forest. You might respond to this place and to the way they do things there by embracing it or resisting it. This reaction will speak of the kind of soul you bring to this encounter, and of your openness to being changed by it.

One of the remarkable things about the story of Naomi and Ruth in the Hebrew scriptures—especially considering the tribal context in which it was written—is that Naomi's sons, who were Hebrews, married Moabite women, while Ruth, a Moabite, married two Hebrew men in succession. This is a story of people who were open to the possibilities that another part of the forest held for them.

Like the characters in the Book of Ruth, some people make deliberate choices that take them from time to time into another part of the forest and into the company of the people who live there. People who live in middle-class suburbs and volunteer in inner-city ministries come into contact with people who live in a very different part of the urban forest. Often the volunteers will undertake their activities with the idea that their role is to give, while the role of those who live in the inner-city community is to receive. But typically, they will find that this other part of the forest is a place for them to learn and grow. They come to recognize the gifts that the people who live there have to offer. Certainly they find—as we often do when we venture into a part of the forest that we have seen only from a distance—that it is more complex on the inside than it appeared from the outside.

Sometimes the steps that take us into another part of the woods are less deliberate. As I was finishing a walk in the woods of a city park, I encountered a man who made his home under the overhang of a building on the edge of the park. He was a modern-day successor to those marginalized beings who, throughout the centuries, have made their home in the forest or on the edge of it. This part of the forest was his home—such as it was—and I felt like an intruder.

Straying into a strange part of the forest—a part that others call home—may prompt feelings of awkwardness, embarrassment, or even shame. You may experience similar feelings about parts of the forest where you occasionally engage in activities that other people might think of as a waste of time. You may keep some of your interests to yourself because "people wouldn't understand."

Other pastimes are kept secret out of a deeper sense of shame. These can include addictions or behaviours that seem at odds with the mainstream of your life—activities involving illicit drugs, for example, or some kinds of sexual behaviour. They may be kept secret, not just because of a fear of the judgmental attitudes of other people, but because at a more basic level you are not happy about them. They represent a captivity to something beyond your control; they create a distance from real intimacy with other people and from the self you want to be. They are a reminder that not all of the other parts of the forest are benign, healthy, or life-giving. Some threaten personal destruction and destruction for people whose lives are affected by such behaviour. These are parts of the forest from which one may need to be delivered.

Other Parts of the Forest: Future Tense

A valid goal with regard to these destructive parts of the forest is to be led out of them. But other parts of the woods may beckon us to a more positive experience. What parts of the forest are waiting for you to explore them? How can you take hold of your future in a way that will open up new areas with life-enriching possibilities?

You may find it helpful to revisit a part of the forest where you once made your home. The "Past Tense" section of this chapter may have prompted you to think of a formative period of your life in which you discovered important things about yourself that you have not thought about for some time. You might want to revisit that place—literally or imaginatively—in order to reconnect with the thoughts and feelings, the people or influences that were significant when you lived there.

On the other hand, if that section reminded you of painful periods in your life, you might want to ask yourself whether you are ready to revisit that part of the forest. The visit might serve to make sense of it and come to terms with it, to confront or forgive the people who hurt you, or to confront or forgive yourself for actions that you have avoided thinking about. At some deep level, you may sense that this period of your past is interfering with your ability to live joyfully and productively in the present. Something may be calling you to return to this part of the woods—not to live there, but to resolve some issues that will allow you to live more fully in the present and the future.

The "Present Tense" section of this chapter may have reminded you of hobbies and interests that you have always wanted to explore. If the "shadow side" of our nature represents neglected aspects of our personalities that need to be acknowledged, perhaps "another part of the forest" refers to the activities we still need to explore if we are to become more creative, well-rounded, and interesting people.

You may have reflected on how broad or narrow is the range of people who are a part of your life. Is your intimate circle made up entirely of people like yourself, sharing your racial background and political outlook, your attitudes and your prejudices? If so, you may want to consider how this situation might change in the future. All too often people find, as they age, that their circle shrinks. They become less tolerant of people who are different from themselves and less willing to consider points of view that do not reinforce their own. If you are to remain open to the possibility of other parts of the forest that wait to be visited, you will have to make deliberate choices about what you read or watch on television, what activities you participate in, and whose company you keep.

It is not too late to make some decisions about how small or big you want your forest to be. It is not too late to decide whether other parts of the forest will be open or closed to you.

For personal reflection or group discussion

1. Have you ever had occasion to visit a part of the forest where you spent an earlier period of your life? What triggered the visit? How did the visit affect you?

2. Thinking of your life as it is now, can you think of a person or a pastime that represents another part of the forest for you? How would your life be different if this person or pastime were not a part of it?

3. What parts of the forest are waiting for you to explore them? Think of as many as you can. Now focus on one that has real potential for exploration in your life, and consider what you are prepared to do to enter that part of the forest.

chapter 10

the sacred grove
finding healing in the woods

I was about to start a hike in the hills above Berkeley, California. On the way to the trailhead, my walk brought me to a stand of California redwoods by the side of the road. Upon entering the grove, the temperature dropped perceptibly within seconds. The feel of the cool air on my skin and the sight of the timeless giant sequoias stretching to the sky produced a sense of awe and peace. I felt soothed, calmed, and quieted. Moments later, I emerged from these woods restored and refreshed for the climb that awaited me.

IN A WOODED TORONTO RAVINE, a sign identifies a fenced plot of new growth as a "natural regeneration area." I was delighted to see this sign, because it reminded me that it is not just flora that requires regeneration. Fauna—including humans—require it, too, and that very ravine provided a time of refreshment for me.

Many of us, in fact, have found the woods to be a "natural regeneration area." The forest is often depicted as a menacing place—and nature can indeed be cruel as well as kind. But when I mention the woods to people, it is often a forest's positive and restorative qualities that come immediately to mind.

The characters who made their way into Shakespeare's Forest of Arden found it to be a place of healing. Their problems were resolved: a usurped duke's duchies were restored and lovesick couples were reunited. Even 400 years ago, *As You Like It* depicted city dwellers who saw the forest as a place that offers refuge and restoration. This attitude continues to be shared by urbanites in our day.

But curiously, living in a society that has allowed itself to be defined for a century now by the automobile, we often resort to automotive metaphors to speak of our need to get a break from an urban, mechanized environment. We describe ourselves as "running on empty," "needing a tune-up," or wanting to "recharge our batteries." Expressions like these suggest a utilitarian approach even to the times we spend communing with nature. These times, apparently, must have a purpose: to re-energize us for more productive work, to restore our flagging creative powers, or to provide respite from the rat race to which we must inevitably return. Such a utilitarian approach to leisure—using rest and relaxation (R&R) merely to equip us for a return to the battle—impedes the ability to simply enjoy time in the natural world.

Many things can hold us back from taking time for ourselves. We may not feel that we deserve the privilege of engaging in an apparently useless activity. If we consider those who take time for themselves lazy, we may not want to open ourselves to the same accusation. A need to feel indispensable can be an impediment; there are people who like to boast about not taking a real holiday for years. Or we may be unable to trust others to look after things properly while we are away. Finally, we may be hindered by a well-founded suspicion that if we let the music stop, if in the midst of frenzied activity we made room for quiet and solitude, we would be confronted by something that we do not want to face.

Any of these impediments may have hindered Jesus' disciples from recognizing their need for respite and restoration. They needed someone else to recognize that need and give them permission to attend to it. At a time when his disciples had been very busy—preaching, casting out demons, anointing the sick—Jesus gave them that permission. Noticing that so much was being demanded of them that "they had no leisure even to eat," he issued an invitation. "Come away to a deserted place all by yourselves," he said, "and rest a while" (Mark 6:31). It was as if he recognized that those who had been engaged in healing needed healing themselves. Or to use the word "cure" in an old-fashioned sense, it could be said that those who had the cure (that is, the spiritual charge) of others needed a cure themselves. Jesus summed up that truism by quoting the proverb (familiar in the *King James Version*): "Physician, heal thyself"; or, as the *New Revised Standard Version* renders it, "Doctor, cure yourself!" (Luke 4:23).

Jesus recognized that the healing and restoration that his friends needed called for a change of scene. They were to go away to a deserted place—to a kind of wilderness, in other words. This time-out required solitude to be effective. And many of us, when we are able to get past the impediments and give ourselves permission to be alone in a deserted place, find ourselves somewhere in the woods.

What—besides ourselves—do we find there? Some of the "re-" words, perhaps: restoration, renewal, regeneration, replenishment, retreat, relaxation, recreation. This prefix indicates bringing something back, establishing again a situation or condition that existed before. This lost state of affairs, it seems, represents the way things are meant to be. We may be exhausted or burnt out, but we are meant to be energized. We may feel empty, but we are meant to be full. We may seem broken, but we are meant to be whole. If we are ill in some way, we are meant to be healed. In fact, if being healed means being made whole or sound again, perhaps the "re-" words are all about healing in one way or another.

Nature's Sacred Spaces

Many people have experienced nature in general and the woods in particular as a source of healing and restoration. The words put to a song by the 17th-century composer Jean-Baptiste Lully express well the healing effect of a woodland walk:

Lonely woods with paths dim and silent,
A haunt of peace for weary-hearted,
There's healing in your shade,
And in your coolness balm.
Here all who seek repose from the world's strife and clamour,
Find a heaven calm and secure,
And go forth strengthened and renewed.[1]

San Diego–based writer Richard Louv warns of the negative consequences if people never have—or never avail themselves of—opportunities to experience the calmness that a forest can impart. In *Last Child in the Woods*, he coined the term "nature-deficit disorder" to describe a condition in children whose difficulty in dealing with stress relates, in his opinion, to a lack of exposure to the world of nature.

For Louv, contact with nature is a requirement of mental health. But it is also a source of *spiritual* health—of renewal and wholeness. In conducting workshops on spirituality, I sometimes ask people what the word "spirituality" suggests to them. For many, spirituality is about connection—connection to something outside or within themselves. And when stress, depression, anxiety, or some other form of dis-ease leaves us feeling disconnected from the environment, from a larger purpose, or from our inner selves, the woods can provide a place for reconnecting.

Many people live and work in environments separated from the earth, which is buried under concrete. We are cut off from the natural world and its life-giving properties. Entering the forest and feeling the earth under our feet can give a sense of connection with creation as we feel "grounded" again.

My brief respite among the California redwoods was a time of awe and wonder. I was overwhelmed by the size of the trees and by their timelessness. They had been there for centuries before I was born and promise to be there long after I die. This setting took me out of my everyday existence and gave a new context to my thoughts about the world and my place in it.

Many people may have felt, when they have spent time in some natural setting, that they are standing on holy ground. The artist Emily Carr found something sacramental in her times in the forest—in the sense that the forest mediated for her something of the divine. In a chapter called "The Piper at the Gates of Dawn" in *The Wind in the Willows*, Kenneth Grahame expresses a belief in the healing power of nature. On an island fringed with willow, silver birch, and alder, Mole and Rat find what Rat calls a holy place, which fills Mole with a sense of awe. The two friends have gone in search of a lost baby otter. Here in this sanctuary, drawn by the sound of pipes played (it turns out) by a benevolent being who has the classical features of the god Pan, they find the baby otter nestling between the god's hooves, safe and sound.

In a wild place, without the benefit—or interference—of any human agency, we too may sense ourselves to be in the presence of the sacred. A piece of creation that is not covered over with signs of human activity may well inspire thoughts of the creator, as the familiar hymn "How Great Thou Art" expresses:

When through the woods and forest glades I wander,
I hear the birds sing sweetly in the trees;
when I look down from lofty mountain grandeur
and hear the brook and feel the gentle breeze.
Then sings my soul…[2]

Something about the natural world draws us out of ourselves and connects us to something larger, something sublime. But it may also send us inward and help us, in the uncluttered quiet, to go more deeply within ourselves. Many people resort to the forest or some other place in nature to find insight into a situation, to sort out a problem, or to refocus their thoughts free from the distractions and demands of everyday life. Ecology writer Wendell Berry finds that it is only as he lies on a bed of newly fallen leaves in the woods that he comes to rest within himself.

Sacred by Association

Perhaps you, like many others, have found a feeling of closeness to nature, to God, or to your own inner being in a forest. Through such an experience, that place may have become holy ground for you. Perhaps the connection was made as you came unawares and for the first time upon some awesome scene and felt your jaw drop in wonder. Another place may have added meaning precisely because you have been there before. Its "holiness" to you is enhanced by its associations with certain people and events. When you feel a need for healing or restoration, this may be a place to which you choose to go.

My brother was living in Winnipeg when our mother died. On a winter's day between her death and her memorial service, he drove up to Victoria

Beach on Lake Winnipeg. This had long been a special place to our mother, where she had spent many happy summer holidays. That day, as my brother walked through the snowy lanes between the stands of trees and strolled along the beach, he could remember and reflect. When it was time to go home, he emerged from the woods with a sense of healing and renewal.

Entire cultures can designate a place as holy ground because of its association with historical events and figures. Jerusalem, Mecca and Medina, Rome and Assisi and Lourdes, Canterbury and Glastonbury: these have become places of pilgrimage because they are hallowed by the past. However, these holy sites often lack the qualities that Jesus had in mind when he invited his disciples to "come away to a deserted place all by yourselves." For one thing, they are rarely deserted. They may provide spiritual renewal, but it is of a kind that is enhanced rather than diminished by the presence of large crowds of pilgrims and tourists. These are not places for people who want to be alone. Also, large human-built structures now cover many of the sites where great things are believed to have happened. Whatever healing elements may have been present when these places were in their natural state have been obscured by architecture, by institutions—and often by commercialism as well.

An exception to this rule can be found in a visit to Iona. Already a pagan holy place when St. Columba brought Christianity there in the sixth century, this remote, small island off the west coast of Scotland retains a relatively unspoilt character. To be sure, there are modest human structures here, some of them dating back centuries. And there are people around, though a visitor is unlikely to feel overwhelmed by crowds. But the windswept island still has the feel of a deserted place where you can be alone with your thoughts and with your soul. Iona has been described as a "thin place," a spot where there is something electric in the atmosphere and the web that divides this world from the other is so tissue-thin that you can almost put your hand through it.

Less celebrated spots—like Hornby Island between Vancouver Island and the mainland of British Columbia—are felt by some to be spiritual places where a sense of healing and renewal can be shared. But beyond the places that are holy to groups of people, most of us can identify a plot of land that is sacred to ourselves, ground that has been hallowed by personal associations. It may be the place where a loved one is buried or where you spent the summer when you were young. Whatever it is, it is a place that feeds your soul because it connects you to things beyond and within you.

Counsellor and oblate Joan Cannon Borton tells of her son, Jim, who each year runs up Mount Adams in the White Mountains of New Hampshire. This pilgrimage, which began simply as a response to a physical challenge, has become an annual event. The run brings him back to the smell of fir trees and the feel of squishy moss underfoot, marking a place of happy childhood memories. The regular return to this holy ground links him to a sense of permanence and stability. Here he has found a personal spiritual place, a place of connection.

Healing Practices

Some of us have places where we go for the sense of connection that feeds our souls and restores our spiritual health. For others, though, a practice may be more important than a place. In fact, even if there are places that we have found to be restorative, limitations of time and money may prevent us from getting to these spots as often as we would like.

I was once asked to lead a men's retreat on the subject of the spirituality of leisure. As the men reflected on their leisure time, I asked them to think of it in terms of "big bits" and "little bits."

The big bits include things that last more than a day or so: vacations, Christmas holidays, sabbaticals, even the weekend retreat at which we were thinking about leisure. It is good have some big bits of leisure in our lives—times that are long enough for us to get away to sanctuaries and sacred places.

But what about the little bits? Have you discovered practices that take minutes or hours, may be done daily, weekly, or monthly, and may not take you far away from home, but that nevertheless take you away from your responsibilities for a time of renewal? Some might think of prayer, meditation, journaling, or recreating a beloved place in nature in their mind's eye; some find refreshment in listening to music or in physical exercise. Others might list recreation that takes place on a golf course or at a card table. I have been known to "lose myself" for a few hours over a jigsaw puzzle. I also frequently take a break from my preoccupations by going for a walk—even if the walk is not always "through the woods."

What is restoring about these activities? They involve stepping out of one's most customary roles. They use our minds or bodies in different ways from the everyday. Or they help us reconnect with a sense of play, something that our workaday lives may not provide for.

There is a significant double meaning in the word "recreation." It is often taken to mean the opposite of work—which it is. But as one of those "re-" words, it can also mean anything that re-creates us, that restores within what has been lost over the course of hours, days, or years.

The big bits that re-create us may take us to sacred places where we can gain a new perspective on our lives and on the world. Similarly, the little bits can provide some distance on issues that may be weighing us down. A woman I know affirms the healing power of water. Soaking in the bathtub provides an opportunity not only to relax and feel renewed, but to sort things out in her life. For her, bath time is almost a sacred ritual—one of those things done regularly in the expectation of something happening, something that can only happen when you place yourself in the presence of the holy and let go.

Some rituals involve "alone time." But restoration and healing can also be found in communal rituals. And for some religions—both ancient and modern—the locale of such rituals is the forest. The rituals of faith can take place in a sacred grove, sometimes among the holy oaks, ivy, and mistletoe. Although the word "sanctuary" now more often refers to a space in a church building than to a space in a forest, public worship with a congregation can support our efforts to gain a different perspective on life, on the world, on what is important. Spirituality is partly about a sense of connection, and that sense can be found by worshipping in community. Even in a space shared with others, we can find "the quiet centre" where we can connect with others, with ourselves, and with the holy.

If spirituality is about connection, that suggests that it is about intimacy and about a willingness to be vulnerable. You may feel an intimate sense of oneness with the holy when you are alone in the woods. But you may also find a profound sense of intimacy in a significant conversation with another person. Intimacy is about a desire to know and be known by another. That other may be God, or another human being.

As we acquire knowledge of one another—as we speak and as we listen— each of us imparts a sense of significance to the other's life. Some people find life partners with whom they can share an intimacy not only of the body, or even of the mind, but of the spirit. Some find a valuable closeness in friend-ship. Any relationship that includes intimate conversations in which we seek guidance, find affirmation, or open our hearts in a spirit of trust and confi-dence can provide moments in which we feel the presence of the holy.

Perhaps the time you have taken to read and reflect on these chapters con-stitutes a spiritual practice in itself. You have taken time away from the other routines of your life. Perhaps this reflects a desire to connect with the things that ground you and give your life shape and meaning.

For personal reflection or group discussion

1. Think of places that are "holy ground" for you. Focusing on just one, what is it that makes this place sacred? Is it associated in your mind with any particular people or events? Does spending time in this place engender any of the "re-" words (refreshed, renewed, regenerated, etc.) in you?

2. Can you identify impediments that interfere with your ability to take time for yourself and for your spiritual needs?

3. When it comes to your need for spiritual renewal and for reconnecting with things within and beyond yourself, have you found any practices to be beneficial? What are they?

chapter 11

the web of life
our place in the forest

A friend and I arranged to meet Marianne Karsh, a guide in spirituality and ecology, at the Rockwood Conservation Area near Guelph, Ontario. As a city-dweller and a rank amateur when it comes to scientific knowledge of forests, I was looking for someone who could help me observe things that I might not otherwise notice or understand in this natural setting. I wanted someone to identify various flora and fauna and explain the connections between them. A professional forester and research scientist with a passion for connecting people with the earth, Marianne seemed to combine the skills and the perspective that I was looking for. On a quiet, overcast day early in the summer, the three of us set off with anticipation into the woods…

THE WOODLAND METAPHORS suggested so far in this book have focused on our individual lives and on the people, events, and influences that affect us in personal ways. Without looking beyond the personal, though, we can get caught in the cult of individualism. Rampant in North America today, this cult may be summed up in the expression "It's all about *me!*"

The forest can speak to us of larger realities. The things that affect and are affected by our lives extend far beyond a small circle of family, friends, and neighbourhood. Similarly, the forest is a major player in the whole ecosphere and has particular functions within it. And the idea of the forest can represent the world of nature in general. Concerns about the health of the forest are symbolic of concerns about the health of the earth itself. "Tree-huggers" are concerned about more aspects of the environment than trees alone. The fate of the Brazilian rain forests—to take one example—has implications that extend far beyond those forests themselves. As go the forests, so goes the planet.

This final chapter challenges you to consider your understanding of human beings in general—and yourself in particular—in relation to the natural world. What is our place in the forest? In nature as a whole?

For example, do you choose to describe the natural world as "creation"? Creation suggests something that was "created" by a "creator." Using such terminology can influence the way we understand our relationship to the world of nature. But before going any further in considering our place in the forest, let us recall how others have understood theirs.

Our Story So Far

We live in a time of serious threats to the world's forests and to the ecosphere itself. Terms that would have meant little or nothing a generation ago—greenhouse effect, acid rain, global warming—have become entrenched in our daily vocabulary. Human beings have gotten ourselves and the world we call home into a serious mess. To many, the problems are practical and need to be approached in a purely practical way.

But as the foregoing chapters have shown, forests also continue to play on the human imagination. They suggest symbolism and invite imagination as we seek to interpret their meaning and comprehend our relationship with them. Since ancient times, forests have played many roles. They have been places to hide (for oneself or for one's enemy), a source of timber and fuel, a playground for the affluent, a home for the marginalized, a place of mystery and menace, and a refuge for the weary.

Often the forest has been understood in merely utilitarian terms. Scripture shows that this approach was common in biblical times. Nearly a millennium before the birth of Jesus, King Solomon turned to the forest as a natural resource to build himself a palace. This great house came to be known as "the House of the Forest of the Lebanon" (1 Kings 7:2)—either because of the cedars of which it was built or perhaps because its rows of cedar pillars looked like a forest.

Centuries later, following the Babylonian captivity, some of the Israelites returned to their homeland to start rebuilding. The Persian King Artaxerxes agreed to a request from a Jewish official named Nehemiah that "Asaph, the keeper of the king's forest" be directed to give him timber to make beams for the gates of the temple fortress and the city wall, as well as for Nehemiah's own house (Nehemiah 2:7–8). Forest management may be thought of as a recent concept, but this man Asaph looked after a royal forest 25 centuries ago!

Forest managers throughout the ages have been charged with controlling the forest and making it productive in ways that would benefit people—or, at least, some people. A swamp (or wetland) that lay in the path of human progress would be drained. A forest that stood in the way of human activity would be cleared.

There are biblical accounts of clearing a forest to expose and conquer an enemy. Jeremiah, for example, compares Egypt's Babylonian adversaries to "those who fell trees. They shall cut down [Egypt's] forest, says the Lord" (Jeremiah 46:22–23). The Assyrian King Sennacherib is described as linking his victory in war with his success in penetrating and destroying the trees of the forest. The king boasts,

> With my many chariots
> I have gone up the heights of the mountains,
> to the far recesses of Lebanon;
> I felled its tallest cedars,
> its choicest cypresses;
> I entered its farthest retreat,
> its densest forest. (2 Kings 19:23)

The power of kings and nations is represented by their ability to penetrate, destroy, or subdue forests. And God's power is sometimes expressed in a similar way. "The voice of the Lord causes the oaks to whirl," says the psalmist, "and strips the forest bare" (Psalm 29:9).

One senses in these passages overtones of testosterone run amok. Some trace those overtones—and a utilitarian understanding of the forest—as far back as an injunction at the end of the first creation story in Genesis. Having crowned creation with human beings, God instructs them to "be fruitful and multiply, and fill the earth and subdue it; and have dominion over the fish of the sea and over the birds of the air and over every living thing" (Genesis 1:28). From passages like this, it would be easy to assume that in the Judeo-Christian tradition, humans have unfettered authority over every being in the world and beyond. It has also been argued that the story implies a hierarchical model of the created order. God is at the top, followed by men, then women, children, animals (from the "higher" to the "lower"), and plant life. At each level, orders are given to those below.

Little in this interpretation prevents the rapacious and greedy exploitation of nature for human use. In fact, from biblical times until quite recently, there has been little thought that, if the forest's ultimate purpose is to provide for human needs, the resource is likely to run out. With good management, the forest could renew itself at a rate that would more than keep pace with human need. But the forest is interconnected with other aspects of nature. What adversely affects the forest also adversely affects the rest of creation.

The potential destructiveness of this model of dominance, a dominance understood to be mandated by God, can be mitigated by seeing human beings as accountable for the way they deal with the rest of creation. In a steward-ship model, humans are responsible to God for their stewardship of creation. They do not merely have dominion over other creatures. They are trustees, occupying a kind of intermediary role between God and creation, caring for the earth and everything in it. They are answerable to God for the quality of their stewardship.

But this model still sees human beings as outside of creation itself. People are to care for the natural world, but are not themselves a part of it. In the stewardship model, it is easy to see other creatures as objects. It is easy to take an anthropocentric (humans-at-the-centre-of-things) view of nature. As God-appointed stewards of creation, humans must know what is best for forests and other elements of nature. The assumption is that forests ultimately exist for the benefit of humankind. Even when a forest is left to itself as much as possible, in this model its pristine beauty exists essentially for us to enjoy.

What is our place in the forest? The prevailing outlook—articulated by philosophers from Plato to Francis Bacon and Descartes and assumed implicitly in Western culture—has considered humans to be essentially different from and superior to the rest of the natural world. This outlook sees forests as having value to humans—whether as sources of fuel, shelter, or oxygen (in the way that the trees of Central Park have been described as the lungs of New York City). But it does not see forests as having intrinsic value in themselves. This outlook, many are coming to see, has led humans and the planet on which we live into serious trouble.

If there are other ways of understanding our place in the forest, it must be admitted that the dire straits in which human beings find themselves have pushed us to consider them. Acid rain affects trees; destruction of forests causes soil erosion and loss of habitat for many species. And when trees no longer shelter a river, the water temperature rises and the stream becomes sluggish and less cleansing. Ultimately, though, it is the way in which these things affect *us* that motivates us to thought and action.

But before thought and action, what about feelings? How do you feel about the state of nature in our day? At various times I have felt guilty and ashamed, angry and sorrowful, confused and resigned. I have even felt alienated and disconnected, and numbed by hopelessness and despair. These emotion-laden words may sound familiar from an earlier discussion in this book—the discussion of grief and loss in Chapter 8.

It is not a new idea that, because of us, something significant has been lost. Human beings are alienated from nature, and nature is no longer our friend. This unpleasant spiritual truth is already present in the story of the Fall in chapter 3 of Genesis. But it is experienced today in a deeper way than ever before. We grieve the loss of the illusion that, because nature is strong, it will survive anything we can do to it. Or perhaps it is the loss of the assumption that human beings are nature's—or God's—little darlings that we lament. Even though the earth may have the capacity to endure, we can no longer assume that humanity will endure with it.

A New Place in the Forest

Of course, the work of grief does not end with an acknowledgement of feelings of sorrow and loss. Grief does not—or should not—end with us mired hopelessly in guilt or despair. There is no empowerment and no life there. To find a new vision for the future—even one triggered in part by self-interest and an instinct for survival—we need to connect with something that can give new life.

The previous chapter considered spirituality as being, at least in part, about a need for connection with something beyond and within ourselves. The forest can help restore us when we feel disconnected, and heal us of our feelings of alienation. The forest may prompt memories of being overwhelmed by a sense of the sublime or of a certain oneness with nature.

Such experiences may be clues to a new way of relating to the natural world. The domination model and even the stewardship model have proven themselves inadequate. Perhaps our instinctive search for wholeness and connection leads to the forest and to the things it can teach.

The trees of the forest—like human beings—are impressive in their unique individuality. But they can also model community. Their root systems often intertwine for mutual support. In relation to other life forms in the forest, trees exist in symbiotic, cooperative relationships. In fact, nearly a century ago, a Russian geographer named Georgy Fedorovich Morozov argued that a forest should not be seen as simply an assortment of individual trees. A forest is a single organism in which cooperation is more evident than competition. Perhaps the living forests of J.R.R. Tolkien's *Lord of the Rings* illustrate this idea.

Using the name of an ancient earth goddess, British scientist James Lovelock developed the Gaia hypothesis, which sees not just the forest but the entire earth as a single organism. Going even further, ecologist Richard St. Barbe Baker refers to nature as a vast sentient being.

These ideas have implications for an understanding of our place in the forest. The sense of a "web of life" that binds the ecosystem together has led some people to rediscover beliefs like animism. An animist outlook, associated with religions that are native to Africa and the Americas, views all living things—including trees—as having souls that should be treated with reverence and respect.

Others are taking a second look at the ancient belief of pantheism, in which God and the universe are identical. In Christian thought, however, God—though active within creation—is also apart from it. A middle path between the two views is proposed by theologians such as Matthew Fox. They use the term "panentheism" to suggest that, though God is not identical with all that is, God is somehow present within all that is.

What does this all mean for those of us who describe nature as "creation"?

Each of these ways of believing suggests that, however the creator may have been involved in initiating creation at a particular point in the past—whether in the ways described in Genesis or by a big bang—the creator continues to live within creation and to relate in intimate ways with everything in it.

Further, these ways of believing claim no special privileges for human beings. We are seen neither as rulers nor as custodians set apart from the rest of the created order. Significantly, over two decades after it authorized "A New Creed," the General Council of The United Church of Canada added a phrase declaring that "We are called…to live with respect in Creation." Perhaps the most telling part of that phrase is the word "in."

Remarkably, not only theologians and mystics are revisiting our ways of relating to this planet and the beings who share it with us. Many scientists, too, are moving beyond a purely mechanistic view of the world and identifying a need to "re-sacralize" nature. The Union of Concerned Scientists in the United States, for example, has called for a recovery of a sense of the sacred in our approach to the natural world. In Canada, David Suzuki and the foundation that bears his name use words that speak of spiritual values: relationship, connection, and interdependence.

During our walk in the woods at the Rockwood Conservation Area, Marianne Karsh told me something of her own story. Trained as a scientist with two degrees in forestry, she began to seek new directions during a period when many research stations were closing at the Canadian Forest Service. Throughout her forestry career, Marianne maintained spiritual interests as well as a love for trees. She realized that her real passion was to help people connect with the earth. To do so on a full-time professional basis, she formed an organization called Arborvitae ("tree of life"), which offers programs for adults and children to nurture spirituality through nature.

Marianne is able to combine her scientific knowledge about the forest with her love of scripture and her sense of the spiritual truths the woods have to teach. Over time she has made connections with a variety of institutions including the Ignatius Jesuit Centre of Guelph, Ontario, where she is Ecology Education Coordinator for a Jesuit collaborative. More remarkably, perhaps, Environment Canada has invited her back to do research on biodiversity and climate change and also to share some aspects of her youth programs. Her journey has come full circle, and she is delighted to be able to integrate her scientific and spiritual interests in all spheres of her life.

The Teachings of the Forest

Through our conversation that day at Rockwood, and through an article that she co-authored with Brian Walsh and Nik Ansell,[1] Marianne shared with me some of the things the forest can teach us—if we listen to it.

Following Jewish theologian Martin Buber, we can be open to the forest's wisdom by learning to regard trees not as objects but as subjects. In other words, by seeing a tree not as an "it" but as a "thou." How would our understanding of our place in the forest change if we imagined not only that we can see the trees, but that the trees can see us? We might be less likely to believe that we know what is best for the forest, and that the forest knows nothing of what it needs—and even of what we need—in order to thrive.

A forest can teach us wisdom through its remarkable ability to survive. All living things die—and certainly each individual tree, plant, and animal in a forest dies. But as a corporate organism, forests are amazingly resilient. They are places where death and decay continually give way to life. Moses could well have borrowed his advice to his people—"choose life" (Deuteronomy 30:19b)—from the forest.

There are valuable lessons to be drawn from this ability. It would be wrong to assume that a forest can take anything we can throw at it, or that we should take its resilience for granted. But I was impressed with a lesson that Marianne recounted from the trees of the Black Forest in Germany. These conifers are suffering from the effects of acid rain. Conditions for their progeny gaining a foothold and surviving are far from favourable. Yet in the last years of their lives, they have been observed to put a tremendous amount of energy into producing an impressive last crop of cones. The prophet Jeremiah bought a field at Anathoth at a time when his country faced destruction, in the hope that one day "houses and fields and vineyards" would again be bought in that land (Jeremiah 32:15). In the same way, present conditions notwithstanding, the trees are expressing an indefatigable hope in the future.

In several scriptural passages, the trees themselves speak to our understanding about our place in the forest. If the instruction to "fill the earth and subdue it" were the only scriptural guidance for understanding our relationship with nature, we might assume that God intends us to have unfettered dominion over a passive, silent, and objectified creation. But when the Hebrew scriptures allow the trees to speak for themselves, they give a very different impression.

A poem in the Book of Isaiah calls on the forest to break into song in praise of God:

Sing, O heavens, for the Lord has done it;
shout, O depths of the earth;
break forth into singing, O mountains,
O forest, and every tree in it! (Isaiah 44:23)

Later the same writer depicts "all the trees of the field" clapping their hands (Isaiah 55:12*b*). In 1 Chronicles, the trees of the forest sing for joy before God:

The trees of the forest [shall] sing for joy
before the Lord, for he comes to judge the earth. (1 Chronicles 16:33)

These words are echoed in Psalm 96:12. God's judgment, it seems, is not something that the trees fear; it is something that they welcome.

Conscious, sentient trees that sing and clap may seem idiosyncratic metaphors. But in the New Testament, the apostle Paul picks up the idea of creation as a sentient being when he speaks of "the whole creation…groaning in labor pains" (Romans 8:22). Passages like these describe creation as active rather than passive. Creation is responsive to the creator and to events within the cosmos, and can feel pain and offer praise.

These passages suggest that creation and created things are capable of relationship with God. That suggestion goes some way toward addressing our own spiritual need for connection with creation and with God. Trees are most often depicted as praising, singing, and rejoicing. They model a particular kind of relationship with the creator—a model that we may be inspired to follow.

Contemplating the future of this planet, it is easy to feel depressed, hopeless, or overwhelmed by the problems and the lack of will on the part of those in power to address them. Some consider the dire situation in which we find ourselves and rage against the greed and short-sightedness of vested interests that have bought us to such a pass. In our outrage, we may imagine that we can dissociate ourselves from the selfishness that has led us here. But we forget the ways in which we are complicit in it. We have benefited—in the short term, at least—from those who have been more directly involved in raping the land and in stripping the forest bare.

Yet, when I asked Marianne Karsh whether she was optimistic about the future, she answered that she was. The way forward, she feels, is not to immobilize people with guilt or blame, but to invite us to embrace a new—yet also, perhaps, old—understanding of our place in the forest. Changed understandings can lead to changed attitudes and changed behaviours.

The forest invites an understanding that responds to our own impulse for life and to our most basic spiritual needs. The forest invites us to connection and relationship, wholeness and creativity, and a heart that knows gratitude and joy.

For personal reflection or group discussion

1. Of the ways of understanding our place in the forest outlined in this chapter (dominion, stewardship, Gaia, animism, pantheism, panentheism, and so on), which comes closest to your understanding?

2. Has your understanding of humanity's place in the ecosphere changed over the years? Why or why not?

3. As you consider the future of this planet, are you hopeful or hopeless? Why?

conclusion

we're not out of the woods yet

AT ONE POINT IN INTO THE WOODS, the Baker's Wife asks, "Who can live in the woods?"[1] Far better, she thinks, to get away from the danger and confusion. The Baker's Wife longs to return to a more straightforward life removed from the challenges and choices that the forest constantly presents.

She might take to heart the advice that Titania, the Queen of the Faeries in *A Midsummer Night's Dream*, gives to Bottom the weaver. "Out of this wood do not desire to go," Titania says. "Thou wilt remain here whether thou wilt or no" (3.1.143).

The things that claim our attention in the forests of imagination may feel like distractions from "real life." We may want to be done with these interruptions and return to life away from the forest, not realizing that it is in the woods that life happens. Forests—fictional and literal—lift up significant aspects of life for us. These aspects of life demand our attention if we are to live our lives with a sense of purpose and self-awareness. Attention to the forest's themes is attention paid to life.

So it may be just as well that we're not out of the woods yet. While we journey through the woods, we still have living to do. We still have opportunities to think about what the woods have to say about our spiritual paths. Robert Frost, in the poem "Stopping by Woods on a Snowy Evening," pauses by the woods for a moment of reflection. We too may pause for a time, and then move forward on our life's journey for whatever miles we have to go before we sleep.

Curiously, though, whatever they have to say about life, the woods are increasingly becoming a place that speaks of death and its aftermath as well. Cremation may be seen as a more environmentally responsible option than traditional embalming and burial in a coffin. But realizing that cremation uses a considerable amount of energy, a growing number of people—particularly in Britain today—are opting for a "green" burial. The body is buried, unembalmed, in a biodegradable coffin in a forest. Even though they are dead, these people are not out of the woods yet.

Woodland burials provide a literal reminder of a spiritual truth. They strikingly demonstrate that it is possible to be at one with the forest and the earth even after death. Illustrating Thomas Saunders' "Native Son," a poem about death and burial, the Canadian artist George Swinton expressed this thought. He portrayed a body in a fetal position enclosed in something like a womb under the ground.

Whatever your belief about the destiny of a disembodied soul or about a bodily resurrection, if your life has a spiritual dimension, so certainly will your death. You may regard the eventual disposal of your body as a purely practical issue. You may try to avoid thinking about what will become of your physical remains when you stop breathing for good. Or you may welcome the idea that the material body that has expressed your presence will—in one way or another—be received by creation itself.

"Earth to earth," the ancient words of committal begin, stating what some would consider a hard if obvious truth, before going on to express the hope of eternal life. But the thought of returning to the earth from which we come, of being rededicated to the creation of which we are a part? There may be hope in that thought as well.

notes

Introduction, pp. 1-6

1. Honoré de Balzac, *Le curé de village* (Paris: Calmann-Lévy, 1893), p. 173. (Author's translation.)
2. Henry David Thoreau, *Walden* (Philadelphia: Courage Books, 1987), p. 60.
3. Corrine J. Saunders, *The Forest of Medieval Romance* (Cambridge: D.S. Brewer, 1993), p. 3.
4. Robert Pogue Harrison, *Forests: The Shadow of Civilization*, © University of Chicago, 1992, p. 82. Used with permission.
5. Reprinted by permission of the publisher from *Six Walks in the Fictional Woods* by Umberto Eco, p. 27, Cambridge, Mass.: Harvard University Press, Copyright ©1994 by the President and Fellows of Harvard College.

Chapter 2, pp. 15-21

1. I KNOW THINGS NOW (FROM "INTO THE WOODS"). Music and Lyrics by STEPHEN SONDHEIM © 1988 RILTING MUSIC, INC. All rights administered by WB MUSIC CORP. All Rights Reserved. Used by Permission by ALFRED PUBLISHING CO., INC.
2. Paulette Bourgeois, *Franklin Is Lost* (Toronto: Kids Can Press, Ltd., 1992), unpaginated.
3. "Adam Lay Y-bounden," *Oxford Carols* (Oxford University Press, 2001).
4. Nathaniel Hawthorne, "Young Goodman Brown," in *The Complete Short Stories of Nathaniel Hawthorne* (Garden City, New York: Hanover House, 1959), p. 255.

Chapter 3, pp. 22-32

1. Reprinted by permission of the publisher from *Six Walks in the Fictional Woods* by Umberto Eco, p. 6, Cambridge, Mass.: Harvard University Press, Copyright ©1994 by the President and Fellows of Harvard College.

Chapter 4, pp. 33-41

1. Bourgeois, *Franklin Is Lost*.

Chapter 5, pp. 42-49

1. Derek G. Evans, "A Clearing in the Forest: An Experience of Discernment in a Time of Personal Transition." Unpublished paper, no date. I am indebted to Derek Evans for his kind permission in using his paper as a resource for some of the ideas in this chapter.

Chapter 7, pp. 60-68

1. Richard Gillard, "The Servant Song," © 1977 Scripture in Song (c/o Integrity Music).
2. Mardi Tindal, *Soul Maps: A Guide to the Mid-life Spirit* (Toronto: United Church Publishing House, 2000), p. 41.
3. *Ibid.*, p. 128.

Chapter 8, pp. 69–78

1. NO ONE IS ALONE (FROM "INTO THE WOODS"). Music and Lyrics by STEPHEN SONDHEIM © 1988 RILTING MUSIC, INC. All rights administered by WB MUSIC CORP. All Rights Reserved. Used by Permission by ALFRED PUBLISHING CO., INC.
2. NO MORE (FROM "INTO THE WOODS"). Music and Lyrics by STEPHEN SONDHEIM © 1988 RILTING MUSIC, INC. All rights administered by WB MUSIC CORP. All Rights Reserved. Used by Permission by ALFRED PUBLISHING CO., INC.

Chapter 10, pp. 88–96

1. Harvey Grace, "Lonely Woods" (London: Novello and Company Limited, n.d.).
2. "How Great Thou Art," Copyright 1953 S.K. Hine. Assigned to Manna Music, Inc., 35255 Brooten Road, Pacific City, OR 97135. Renewed 1981 by Manna Music, Inc. All rights reserved. Used by permission. (ASCAP)

Chapter 11, pp. 97–106

1. Brian Walsh, Marianne B. Karsh, Nik Ansell, "Trees, Forestry and the Responsiveness of Creation" in *Cross Currents*, Summer 1994, Vol. 44, Issue 2, p. 149, 14 pp.

Conclusion, pp. 107–108

1. MOMENTS IN THE WOODS (FROM "INTO THE WOODS"). Music and Lyrics by STEPHEN SONDHEIM © 1988 RILTING MUSIC, INC. All rights administered by WB MUSIC CORP. All Rights Reserved. Used by Permission by ALFRED PUBLISHING CO., INC.